Understanding Charter Damages

UNDERSTANDING CHARTER DAMAGES

The Judicial Evolution of a Charter Remedy

W.H. Charles

IRWIN LAW

Understanding Charter Damages: The Judicial Evolution of a Charter Remedy

Published in 2016 by

Irwin Law Inc.
14 Duncan Street
Suite 206
Toronto, ON
M5H 3G8

www.irwinlaw.com

ISBN: 978-1-55221-390-2
e-book ISBN: 978-1-55221-391-9

Library and Archives Canada Cataloguing in Publication

Charles, W. H. R., author
Understanding Charter damages : the judicial evolution of a charter remedy / W.H. Charles.

Includes bibliographical references and index.
Issued in print and electronic formats.

ISBN 978-1-55221-390-2 (paperback).—ISBN 978-1-55221-391-9 (pdf)

1. Damages—Canada. 2. Canada. Canadian Charter of Rights and Freedoms. I. Title.

KE1305 C43 2016	342.7108'8	C2016-900135-0
KF1321 C43 2016		C2016-900136-9

Canada Ontario
Ontario Media Development Corporation
Société de développement de l'industrie des médias de l'Ontario

Printed and bound by CPI Group (UK) Ltd, Croydon, CR0 4YY

1 2 3 4 5 20 19 18 17 16

To my dear wife, Dorine,
without whose enduring patience and support
this book would not have been written.

Table of Contents

Acknowledgements

I want to recognize with sincere gratitude the contributions made by the following persons to the publication of *Understanding* Charter *Damages*: members of the law library staff of the Schulich School of Law and, in particular, David Michels, Mark Lewis, and Anne-Marie White for their help with legal research and data collection; Andrea Davidson and Molly Ross for their transcription of the many drafts of the manuscript; John Sawicki and Alisa Posesorski of the editorial staff of Irwin Law for their helpful insights and attention to detail; and Jeffrey Miller of Irwin Law for making publication possible.

Preface

It has more than been thirty years since the *Constitution Act, 1982*[1] was passed by the British Parliament. Part I of that Act contains the *Canadian Charter of Rights and Freedoms*,[2] which establishes for all Canadians recognition and protection of certain basic rights and freedoms considered to be essential to the maintenance of our free and democratic society. One section of the *Charter*, section 24, entitled "Enforcement," provides that any person or group whose rights have been denied or infringed upon by state action can apply to a court for a remedy deemed by the court to be "appropriate and just in the circumstances." Section 24(1) does not list specific remedies that may qualify as appropriate and just. Instead, a broad discretion is conferred upon the court to determine what specific remedy would be considered by the court to be suitable in the circumstances of the individual case.

Remedies can be either defensive, as in the case of a stay of proceedings, or affirmative, as in the case of an injunction or damages, which require further positive action.[3] In addition to damages, an injunction, or a stay, there are a variety of other potential remedies, such as a declaration, costs, an acquittal, or a prerogative writ in the form of certiorari, mandamus, prohibition, or *habeas corpus*.[4] Exclusion of evidence as a remedy is specifically provided

---

1 Being Schedule B to the *Canada Act 1982* (UK), 1982, c 11.

2 Part I of the *Constitution Act, 1982*, *ibid* [*Charter*].

3 This distinction is explained more fully by Professor Ken Cooper-Stephenson in his book Charter *Damages Claims* (Toronto: Carswell, 1990) at 4–6.

4 A more complete list would include interpretive remedial actions such as "reading down," severance, nullification, constitutional exemption, and

for by section 24(2) of the *Charter*. Although damages are not specifically referred to in section 24(1), there are a couple of good reasons to support the assumption that Parliament intended damages to be a remedy available to courts to redress violations of the *Charter*. First, damages or money compensation has historically been the primary remedy used by common law courts to redress civil wrongs. The fact that common law damages are automatically available once proof of wrongdoing has been established demonstrates their importance as a remedy. Although *Charter* damages would not be automatically available, given the judicial discretion provided by section 24(1), this would not rule them out as a potential remedy. A second reason for believing that damages were intended to be available as a *Charter* remedy is that they have already been accepted as a suitable remedy in quasi-constitutional human rights codes and by the Supreme Court of the United States in American constitutional law.[5]

There are, however, equally strong reasons to suppose that Parliament did not favour damages as a *Charter* remedy. Foremost among these is the ever-present concern for a flood of applicants requesting damages once it becomes apparent that they are available.[6] This concern would be well-founded in a society or culture that is more than ready to lay blame on others, and especially the government, for every negative effect suffered. And then there is concern for the economic impact of many, and perhaps large, damages awards on the public purse.[7] Some might argue that such damages awards should be accepted as a necessary cost of the government enterprise conducted for the well-being of all taxpayers and as justifiable

---

extension. In addition, there is remedial relief in the criminal law context, including dismissal of charges, reduction of sentence, release of prisoner, and quashing of search warrants, as well as a variety of miscellaneous orders. Oonagh E Fitzgerald lists potential remedies in her publication *Understanding* Charter *Remedies: A Practitioner's Guide* (Toronto: Carswell, 1994) (loose-leaf 1995 revision 1) at 3-11 and 5-2.

5 Professor Cooper-Stephenson makes this point, above note 3 at 1.

6 See Carol Harlow, "Damages and Human Rights" [2004] *New Zealand Law Review* 429 at 430, who argues that "[s]uccessful damages actions do open floodgates."

7 In a seminal article discussing *Charter* damages, Professor Marilyn L Pilkington briefly mentions this concern: "Damages as a Remedy for Infringement of the *Canadian Charter of Rights and Freedoms*" (1984) 62:4 *Canadian Bar Review* 517 at 519. For a more extensive discussion of the problem, see Walter E Dellinger, "Of Rights and Remedies: The Constitution as a Sword" (1972) 85 *Harvard Law Review* 1532 at 1533, quoted in Harlow, above note 6 at 431.

expenditures to protect rights that are fundamental.[8] A third concern of Parliament might have been the possible detrimental effect of damages awards upon the desire or willingness of government officials to carry out their duties in an effective way.[9] Without a clear direction in section 24 as to the appropriateness of damages as a *Charter* remedy, courts could only speculate about Parliament's actual intention and, perhaps, take into account some of the policy considerations discussed above when faced with an application for *Charter* damages.[10]

Even if courts were prepared to accept *Charter* damages as a suitable *Charter* remedy, and if the violation of a *Charter* right were proven, there were still important issues to be faced. The first and most basic problem was to determine or identify the circumstances that would warrant an award of *Charter* damages. Not surprisingly, the answer here would depend upon a number of relevant factors including the nature of the defendant's conduct and mental state, whether the claimant had suffered real tangible loss or harm of some type, what other remedies were available to the claimant, and which remedy would provide the most effective means of vindicating the right or rights violated and, perhaps, provide general deterrence. Additionally, there was the question whether an award of damages would be effective without interfering disproportionally with the implementation of government policy. Finally, if damages were to be awarded, how would the quantum be set?[11]

---

8 See Pilkington, above note 7 at 576.

9 This concern is frequently raised in the context of the Crown immunity defence. Professor Pilkington also mentions it briefly, *ibid* at 519.

10 Had the courts examined the legislative history of s 24, they would have discovered several earlier versions with different wording. The first version of s 24 authorized the court to enforce *Charter* rights "by means of a declaration of the court or by means of an injunction or similar relief, accordingly as the circumstances require": Canada, *The Constitutional Amendment Bill: Text and Explanatory Notes* (Ottawa: Government of Canada, 1978) at 12, cited in WHR Charles, Thomas A Cromwell, & Keith B Jobson, *Evidence and the* Charter of Rights and Freedoms (Toronto: Butterworths, 1989) at 211. A second version of s 24 authorized a claimant "to apply to a court of competent jurisdiction to obtain relief or remedy by way of declaration, injunction, damages or penalty, as may be appropriate and just in the circumstances" (Charles, Cromwell, & Jobson, *ibid* at 218). Significantly, in this second version of s 24(1), damages were specifically authorized as a *Charter* remedy. See also Anne McLellan & Bruce P Elman, "The Enforcement of the *Canadian Charter of Rights and Freedoms*: An Analysis of Section 24" (1983) 21 *Alberta Law Review* 205.

11 One early commentator suggests four situations where damages may be an appropriate remedy: where (1) real harm has occurred, (2) a *Charter* violation

From the outset, academic commentators in constitutional law texts[12] and articles in major periodicals[13] speculated about damages as a potential remedy or assumed it would be available as such. The author of a seminal law review article declared that, in addition to common law remedies, there was a need for a separate remedy in the form of *Charter* damages to vindicate *Charter* rights.[14] The question was whether courts would agree. The survey in this book shows that trial courts have had little difficulty assuming that *Charter* damages were intended to be one of the remedies that a court may provide to redress *Charter* wrongs. By contrast, the questions that invariably followed from this assumption posed greater difficulty for the courts.

In general, they appear to have reacted moderately sympathetically to *Charter* damages claims. Trial courts, in the early years, did their best to discover and carry out what they thought was the legislative intent of section 24(1) and to give the intended meaning to the broad language of that section. However, lower-court decisions during these years reveal quite a variety of approaches and results.[15] This is not surprising given the absence of any broad authoritative direction from a higher court.

The Supreme Court of Canada eventually addressed this lack of direction in 2010 in the British Columbia case of *Vancouver (City) v Ward*.[16] In this case, the unanimous decision of the Court was written by McLachlin CJ, who decided that Canadians should have the right to seek monetary compensation if their constitutional rights have been violated. Ironically, or perhaps appropriately, the claimant in this case was a lawyer. But not only did the Supreme Court affirm what lower courts had themselves decided, not always with consistency or confidence, that *Charter* damages were an appropriate remedy, the Supreme Court went further by providing a broad

---

has been suffered but no real harm has resulted, (3) other defensive remedies "would interfere unduly in government policy," or (4) government action was so egregious that punitive damages were required (Fitzgerald, above note 4 at 5-57).

12 See, for example, WS Tarnopolsky & GA Beaudoin, eds, *Canadian Charter of Rights and Freedoms* (Toronto: Carswell, 1982).

13 See, for example, Pilkington, above note 7; McLellan & Elman, above note 10. The latter categorically state, *ibid* at 221, "Certainly one of the remedies available to a Superior Court under Section 24(1) will be damages."

14 Pilkington, above note 7.

15 As the Supreme Court was to observe in 1994, there was a lack of developed *Charter* jurisprudence: *RJR – MacDonald Inc v Canada* (AG), [1994] 1 SCR 311 at 342 [*RJR – MacDonald*].

16 2010 SCC 27 [*Ward*].

analytical framework within which lower courts could work in reaching their decisions.

It is important to appreciate that before the *Ward* decision, the Supreme Court of Canada had rendered a number of decisions that involved the application of section 24(1). Some were concerned with the relationship between sections 52(1) and 24(1) in terms of remedies available.[17] Other decisions focused upon the issue of proper jurisdiction[18] or the power of the court to provide a specific remedy.[19] Still other cases grappled with the applicability and scope of the common law defence of qualified immunity[20] or provincial limitation statutes.[21] However, no previous decision of the Supreme Court had dealt with damages as an acceptable *Charter* remedy in the same comprehensive way as did the decision in *Ward*.[22]

This book endeavours to provide some context or background for the *Ward* decision by looking at a fairly comprehensive sampling of lower-court

---

17 See *R v Mills*, [1986] 1 SCR 863 [*Mills*]; *R v Rahey*, [1987] 1 SCR 588; *Schachter v Canada*, [1992] 2 SCR 679; *R v Ferguson*, 2008 SCC 6.

18 See *Weber v Ontario Hydro*, [1995] 2 SCR 929; *Nova Scotia (Workers Compensation Board) v Martin*, 2003 SCC 54; *Blencoe v British Columbia (Human Rights Commission)*, 2000 SCC 44; *Mills*, above note 17; *R v Big M Drug Mart*, [1985] SCR 295 (jurisdiction of provincial criminal courts to grant remedies for breach of *Charter* rights); *Ontario v 974649 Ontario Inc*, 2001 SCC 81 (authority of a justice of the peace sitting as a trial judge under the *Provincial Offences Act*, RSO 1990, c P.33).

19 As in *Doucet-Boudreau v Nova Scotia (Minister of Education)*, 2003 SCC 62, where the issue was whether the trial judge had the jurisdiction to issue orders to the government of Nova Scotia requiring it to build a French-speaking school in a certain part of Nova Scotia and to report back to the court on its progress.

20 See *Guimond v Quebec (AG)*, [1996] 3 SCR 347; *Mackin v New Brunswick (Minister of Finance)*, 2002 SCC 13; *Pearson v Canada*, [2008] SCCA No 299, aff'g 2007 FCA 380, Linden JA, though not a fully reasoned judgment on the point of qualified immunity.

21 See *Kingstreet Investments Ltd v New Brunswick (Finance)*, 2007 SCC 1 at para 60; *Ravndahl v Saskatchewan*, 2009 SCC 7 at para 27 (limitation statute applies to a personal remedy claim for damages under s 24(1) but does not apply to the remedy involved in s 52(1)).

22 *Ward*, above note 16. As a former legal academic and retired justice of the Federal Court of Appeal observed, the "Supreme Court has hinted in several early cases that this [s 24(1)] was an avenue of redress that was potentially available in addition to other commonly used constitutional remedies, but the Court never seemed to get the chance to order such a remedy": Allen M Linden, "*Charter* Damage Claims: New Dawn or Mirage?" (2012) 39:4 *Advocates' Quarterly* 426 at 427.

and Supreme Court decisions rendered in the twenty-seven years before *Ward*.[23] Chapter 1 covers lower-court decisions for the period 1984 to 1994.[24] The cut-off date for this period has been chosen because it marks the date of the first real discussion of *Charter* damages as a remedy under section 24(1) by the Supreme Court.[25] The second period, 1995 to 2010, is slightly longer and takes us up to the Supreme Court decision in *Ward*. Chapter 2 discusses the significance of Supreme Court decisions in the first period, 1984 to 1994,[26] while Chapter 3 covers lower-court decisions during the period 1995 to 2010, including the Court of Appeal decision in *Ward*.[27] Chapter 4 covers Supreme Court decisions rendered during the period 1995 to 2010.[28] The hope is that this arrangement will give readers some sense of the issues surrounding the application of section 24(1) and, in particular, the remedy of *Charter* damages, which lower courts struggled with, as well as a sense of how much direction and guidance emanated from the Supreme Court specifically from 1984 to 2010. In addition, the review of lower-court decisions provides data regarding the rate of success in *Charter* damages claims, some sense of why, in a significant number of cases, the claimant failed, the range of damages awards, and the approach of trial courts as contrasted with that of courts of appeal, as well as the emergence of specific troublesome issues. Chapter 5 explores the role of tort damages in the evolution of *Charter* damages while Chapter 6 provides an extensive assessment of the *Ward* decision itself.[29] Chapter 7 examines the effect of the *Ward* decision upon subsequent lower-court decisions dealing with issues related to *Charter* damages during the period 2010 to the end of 2014.[30] Finally, Chapter 8 provides a general summary of the data and conclusions.

---

23 The seventy-one cases involved include decisions of provincial and federal trial courts, provincial and federal appeal courts, and the Supreme Court. The cases are listed in Appendix 1, which provides not only the style of cause and legal citations for each case but also specifies whether the claim for *Charter* damages was accepted and, if so, information regarding award amounts and the type of compensation awarded.

24 See Appendix 1, cases 1–21.

25 This discussion occurred in *RJR – MacDonald*, above note 15.

26 For a list of these cases, see Appendix 3.

27 2009 BCCA 23. For a list of these cases, see Appendix 1, cases 22–71.

28 For a list of these cases, see Appendix 4.

29 *Ward*, above note 16.

30 See Appendix 1, cases 72–104.

Chapter 1

The First Period of Evolution

1984–94

A. SHORT SUMMARY OF DATA REGARDING TRIAL AND APPEAL COURT DECISIONS

A sampling of seventy-one cases comprising eighty-one judgments of provincial and federal trial and appellate courts shows that damages were awarded under section 24(1) of the *Charter*[1] in 35 percent of the cases where they were claimed during the period 1984 to 2010.[2] Trial courts awarded damages in 40 percent of the cases[3] while appeal courts were less generous, awarding damages under section 24(1) in only 33 percent of the cases.[4] The lower success rate at the appeal level is not altogether surprising given the more cautious approach of higher courts to new legal developments generally.

Although Parliament gave the courts broad authority in section 24(1) to provide remedies that are "appropriate and just in the circumstances," it failed to provide them with more specific directions or guidance as to the criteria to be applied when exercising their newly provided wide discretion. Theoretically, courts of appeal are considered to have more time to consider the jurisprudential landscape and thereby provide a road map for the lower trial courts. A review of *Charter* damages cases in the first eleven years[5] indicates not a single provincial or federal court of appeal decision providing

---

1 *Canadian Charter of Rights and Freedoms*, Part I of the *Constitution Act, 1982*, being Schedule B to the *Canada Act 1982* (UK), 1982, c 11 [*Charter*].

2 These cases are collected in Appendix 5 for ease of reference together with award amounts.

3 These cases are listed in Appendix 6.

4 These cases are listed in Appendix 7.

5 See Appendix 1, cases 1–21.

any kind of guidance or analytical framework that would assist trial courts in the application of section 24(1).

It would be 1994 before Canada's highest court would have the opportunity to provide some of the needed specifics.[6] Before proceeding to a review of specific lower-court decisions handed down during the period 1984 to 1994 and the way that those courts interpreted the application of section 24(1), we should consider the impact of section 52(1) of the *Constitution Act, 1982*[7] and its relationship to section 24(1) of the *Charter*. These two provisions both involve constitutional remedies, and their interaction was the issue in several cases that found their way to the Supreme Court of Canada early on.

B. RELATIONSHIP BETWEEN SECTIONS 24(1) AND 52(1)

At first glance, sections 24(1) and 52(1) appear to have different functions and objectives. Section 52(1) of the *Constitution Act, 1982* provides that laws found to be inconsistent with the *Charter* by a court have no force or effect to the extent of that inconsistency.[8] This power to render laws null and void is nonspecific in nature and provides the courts with a remedy that has broad application. Section 24(1) of the *Charter*, on the other hand, appears to give the court the discretion to provide, on a case-by-case basis, an "appropriate and just" remedy in any situation where a person's rights or freedoms as guaranteed by the *Charter* have been denied. Violation of rights or freedoms can occur as a result of the enactment of an unconstitutional statutory provision or statute or by the unconstitutional acts of government agents acting under lawful legislative schemes or provisions. In other words, section 24(1) can apply to situations where the law that government agents are acting under is lawful or constitutionally valid but where the actions of the agents are not.

As noted above, if a law or legislative provision is challenged and found to violate constitutional rights, it can be declared unconstitutional by the court. The judicial declaration of invalidity pursuant to section 52(1) is a formal remedy and, from a functional perspective, creates an area of remedial

---

6 See *RJR – MacDonald Inc v Canada (AG)*, [1994] 1 SCR 311 [*RJR – MacDonald*].

7 Being Schedule B to the *Canada Act 1982* (UK), 1982, c 11.

8 For what appears to be the latest word on the subject, see *R v Ferguson*, 2008 SCC 6 at paras 35 and 58–63, McLachlin CJ. The issue had also been considered and discussed in earlier Supreme Court decisions including *Schachter v Canada*, [1992] 2 SCR 679 [*Schachter* SCC]; *Guimond v Quebec (AG)*, [1996] 3 SCR 347; *Mackin v New Brunswick (Minister of Finance)*, 2002 SCC 13.

overlap with section 24(1) in the sense that a court using the latter provision can theoretically provide a remedy in the form of either a declaration of invalidity or damages. The specific question that has arisen in the cases is whether it is possible or permissible for a court to issue concurrent remedies, one pursuant to section 52(1) in the form of a declaration and one via section 24(1) in the form of damages? The question was first raised by the Federal Court of Appeal in 1990 in the case of *Schachter v Canada*[9] and later answered by the Supreme Court of Canada in 1992.[10]

C. LOWER-COURT DAMAGES AWARDS 1984–94

Lower-court decisions in response to applications under section 24(1) for *Charter* damages as a remedy began appearing in 1984. Some were decisions by provincial and federal trial courts, and there were a smaller number of decisions by provincial and federal courts of appeal as well. This study has selected for examination a fairly comprehensive sample of twenty-one cases, comprising twenty-one trial court decisions and seven court of appeal decisions, all decided between 1984 and 1994.[11] They represent the first eleven years of section 24(1) jurisprudence. The year 1994 is also significant because it was the first time that the Supreme Court of Canada had an opportunity to provide lower courts with any degree of guidance as to the role of damages as a *Charter* remedy.[12]

The review of twenty-eight decisions will focus on the following issues: (1) the success and rejection rate at both trial and appeal court levels, (2) reasons for rejection, (3) amount of awards, (4) *Charter* sections involved, (5) degree of defendant's fault required, (6) type of damages awarded, (7) punitive damages, and (8) recurring problems.

1) Success Rate

The claimant was awarded damages in 38 percent of the twenty-one cases (eight out of twenty-one).[13] This means a rejection rate of 62 percent. The

9 (1990), 66 DLR (4th) 635 [*Schachter* FCA].

10 *Schachter* SCC, above note 8.

11 See Appendix 1.

12 See *RJR – MacDonald*, above note 6.

13 These cases include *Crossman v Canada*, [1984] 1 FC 681 (TD) [*Crossman*]; *R v BB* (1986), 69 AR 203 (Prov Ct) [*BB*]; *Lord v Allison* (1986), 3 BCLR (2d) 300 (SC) [*Lord*]; *R v F(RG)* (1991), 90 Nfld & PEIR 113 (Nfld SC) [*F(RG)*]; *Rollinson v Canada*, [1991] 3 FC 70 (TD) [*Rollinson*]; *Blouin v Canada* (1991), 51 FTR 194

high rejection rate is significantly affected by the fact that six of the seven claims for damages that went to the court of appeal level were rejected.[14] If the rate of success is measured by only trial awards, the success rate increases to 52 percent, and the rejection rate decreases to 48 percent. The impressive display of consistency at the court of appeal level was achieved by both provincial and federal courts of appeal. But however consistent the court results might seem, the reasons for appellate rejections vary considerably. In two cases, the court of appeal found no *Charter* violations, and therefore there was no need to consider a remedy.[15] In two other cases, the court of appeal required proof of malice or *mala fides* on the part of the government official involved as a prerequisite to a damages award.[16] In one case, the court refused a damages award because no actual or real harm or damage had been established.[17] The final case of the six was decided negatively on a procedural point.[18] Seven of the twenty-one cases involved decisions of a federal court.[19] Of the remaining fourteen provincial court cases, five (36 percent) involved decisions of British Columbia courts.[20]

(TD) [*Blouin*]; *Lewis v Burnaby School District No 41* (1992), 71 BCLR (2d) 183 (SC) [*Lewis*]; *Patenaude v Roy* (1994), 23 DLR (4th) 78 (Que SC), var'd 1994 CanLII 6107 (Que CA) [*Patenaude*]. Award amounts can be found in Appendix 5.

14 These cases were *Collin v Lussier*, [1983] 1 FC 218 (TD), rev'd in part [1985] 1 FC 124 (CA) [*Collin*]; *S Bertram Miller Ltd v Canada*, [1985] 1 FC 72 (TD), rev'd [1986] 3 FC 291 (CA), leave to appeal to SCC refused (1986), 75 NR 159n [*S Bertram Miller*]; *Freeman v West Vancouver (District)* (1992), 19 BCAC 81 (CA), leave to appeal to SCC refused (1993), 77 BCLR (2d) xxxi [*Freeman*]; *Stenner v British Columbia (Securities Commission)* (1993), 23 Admin LR (2d) 247 (SC), aff'd (1996), 141 DLR (4th) 122 (BCCA) [*Stenner*]; *McGillivary v New Brunswick* (1993), 140 NBR (2d) 365 (QB), aff'd (1994), 116 DLR (4th) 104 (CA) [*McGillivary*]; *Crown Trust Co v Ontario* (1986), 54 OR (2d) 79 (Div Ct) [*Crown Trust*].

15 *Freeman*, *ibid*; *S Bertram Miller*, *ibid*.

16 *Stenner*, above note 14; *McGillivray*, above note 14.

17 *Vespoli Precision Mechanics Ltd v Canada* (1984), 12 CRR 185 (FCA) [*Vespoli*].

18 *Collin*, above note 14.

19 *Crossman*, above note 13; *Collin*, above note 14; *Vespoli*, above note 17; *S Bertram Miller*, above note 14; *Lagiorgia v Canada*, [1985] 1 FC 438 (TD), rev'd in part [1987] 3 FC 28 (CA), leave to appeal to SCC refused (1988), 61 CR (3d) xxviii [*Lagiorgia*]; *Rollinson*, above note 13; *Blouin*, above note 13.

20 *Lord*, above note 13; *Bauder v Wilson* (1988), 43 CRR 149 (BCSC) [*Bauder*]; *Freeman*, above note 14; *Lewis*, above note 13; *Stenner*, above note 14.

2) Reasons for Rejection Generally

The most prevalent reason for judicial rejection of damages claims was the court's insistence that the claimant prove *mala fides*, malice, or wilful violation of *Charter* rights.[21] A second significant reason for rejection was double recovery in cases where the claimant could also prove tortious acts on the part of the government and was entitled to common law tort damages.[22] Failure of the claimant to prove a *Charter* violation due to the lack of a causal connection was not a factor at all.

3) Amount of Awards

During the first eleven years of *Charter* litigation the average award, including both compensatory and punitive damages, was $16,687. This average is inflated considerably by an award of $100,000 by the Quebec Court of Appeal in *Patenaude v Roy*.[23] The trial court in that case had awarded the claimant $50,000 in *Charter* damages, but the Court of Appeal increased the award to $100,000 making it clear in its judgment that the added $50,000 represented punitive damages. If the *Patenaude* award is excluded from the calculation, the average *Charter* damages award decreases to $4,785.[24] The highest *Charter* damages award made by a non-Quebec court was $18,500, awarded by the Federal Court – Trial Division in *Collin v Lussier*.[25] This award comprised $11,000 in compensatory damages to cover real tangible losses and $7,500 in punitive damages. Punitive damages awards in other cases ranged from $500[26] to $5,000.[27] The average *Charter* damages award made by federal trial courts was $8,970.

---

21 In 38 percent of the cases where *Charter* damages claims were rejected, the court required this higher standard of fault on the part of the defendant. In 70 percent of the claims rejected at the trial level, this higher standard was required.

22 This basis for rejection accounted for 23 percent of the rejection cases, including *Bauder*, above note 20, *Breen v Saunders* (1986), 71 NBR (2d) 404 (QB) [*Breen*], and *Charters v Harper* (1987), 79 NBR (2d) 28 (QB) [*Charters*], all trial court decisions.

23 *Patenaude*, above note 13.

24 See Appendix 5 for damages award amounts in individual cases.

25 *Collin*, above note 14.

26 *Crossman*, above note 13.

27 *Freeman*, above note 14.

4) *Charter* Sections Involved

Of the cases in the first eleven years, 57 percent involved either section 7 or 8 of the *Charter*.[28] This is understandable given the fact that many of the early *Charter* cases involved criminal law issues in which the *Charter* applicant raised questions about the legality of state actions in criminal prosecutions. Counsel for the defendant in criminal cases frequently made arguments alleging illegal arrest and detention or illegal search and seizure. The remaining 43 percent of cases involved section 10 (three cases), sections 15 and 9 (two cases each), and sections 2(b) and 11(b) (one case each).[29]

There appears to be no correlation between the section involved and the rate of rejection. In this regard, the trial decisions involving section 7 or 8 are almost equally divided in the results. At the court of appeal level, on the other hand, all decisions involving section 7 or 8 resulted in a rejection of the damages requested.[30]

5) Fault Requirement

In Canadian law generally, the fault standard varies according to the area of law involved. For example, in the area of human rights law, courts tend to apply the high standard of strict liability, while courts deciding administrative law matters tend to apply a mixture of standards: regarding liability issues, courts seem to require malice, but they apply the standard of reasonableness when hearing judicial review cases.[31] Tort law applies a wide range of fault concepts including negligence, strict liability, and malice, which involves intentional conduct and improper purpose directed to the plaintiff, as well as intentional acts *simpliciter*. Courts in tort cases applying a strict liability standard often raise the question whether real or actual damages are required, particularly if there is to be a substantial award given.

In seven of the twenty-one cases decided between 1984 and 1994, the courts applied the very high fault standard of malicious conduct as the ne-

---

28 These cases are listed in Appendix 8.

29 Section 10: *Crossman*, above note 13; *Lord*, above note 13; *Blouin*, above note 13. Section 15: *Lewis*, above note 13; *Stenner*, above note 14. Section 9: *Blouin*, above note 13; *Freeman*, above note 14. Section 2(b): *Lord*, above note 13. Section 11(b): *Moore v Ontario (AG)*, [1990] OJ No 3433 (Dist Ct) [*Moore*].

30 *Vespoli*, above note 17; *McGillivary*, above note 14; *Stenner*, above note 14; *S Bertram Miller*, above note 14; *Collin*, above note 14.

31 See Ken Cooper-Stephenson, Charter *Damages Claims* (Toronto: Carswell, 1990) at 164.

cessary threshold for an award of *Charter* damages under section 24(1).[32] This number represents one third of the cases decided and 54 percent of the rejected cases.

The defendant raised the defence of qualified immunity in nine cases during the period, and the court refused to apply or recognize the defence in two of those cases.[33] When the defence of qualified immunity is raised and accepted by the court, the claimant is forced to establish lack of good faith or *mala fides* on the part of the Crown or its agents. In the two cases[34] where the defence was raised but where the courts refused to give effect to it, there were other policy considerations that the courts considered more important than protecting the Crown from liability.

By contrast, in fourteen cases (two-thirds)[35] trial courts appeared willing to apply a less onerous fault standard as a prerequisite for a *Charter* damages award. In nine cases,[36] intentional torts were involved, and either the court specifically discussed the tortious conduct, such as assault, battery, or false imprisonment, or it could be reasonably inferred from the court judgment that fault in the form of intentional tortious conduct was sufficient. In two cases,[37] the court suggested that negligence, carelessness, or inadvertence might be sufficient. And in three cases, the court awarded damages without any apparent need for fault to be established at all.[38] In two of these cases,[39] the state officials had acted in reliance upon statutory provisions later declared to be unconstitutional. In these latter two cases, there was no intention to violate *Charter* rights or even negligence.

The overall picture painted in the first eleven years of *Charter* damages awards shows that in a significant majority of cases the trial courts were prepared to award *Charter* damages in situations where the Crown or state officials had not acted maliciously. The higher standard was still applied in a significant percentage of the cases (one-third). Clearly the pleading of qualified immunity as a defence forced courts to specifically consider whether the high standard of fault should be required, but, as shown above, several courts were prepared to ignore the defence and the higher standard when necessary.

---

32 For a list of these cases, see Appendix 12.

33 *Lewis*, above note 13; *S Bertram Miller*, above note 14.

34 *Ibid.*

35 See Appendix 13.

36 See *ibid.*

37 *Lord*, above note 13; *F(RG)*, above note 13.

38 *Blouin*, above note 13; *Lewis*, above note 13; *S Bertram Miller*, above note 14.

39 *Lewis*, above note 13; *S Bertram Miller*, above note 14.

6) Type of Damages Awarded

Not surprisingly, compensatory damages were the most frequently awarded type of damages (eight cases, including one global award),[40] but perhaps surprising was the almost equal number of awards for punitive damages (seven cases).[41] In some cases, the punitive damages award was made in addition to a compensatory award,[42] but in other cases, it was the only damages award.[43] Aggravated damages were awarded in two cases.[44]

As already noted, there were three cases where the courts appeared to have awarded damages without fault having been proven on the part of the state.[45] Only one of these cases involved no actual economic loss.[46] In this case, an illegal search affected the plaintiff's dignity and caused humiliation; hence the award could be considered an example of damages *per se*. In another of the three cases, although there was actual loss of income due to a forced retirement, the court stated that the award was intended to vindicate the plaintiff's *Charter* rights.[47]

7) Punitive Damages

In the vast majority of cases where courts awarded punitive damages, it was on their own initiative. In only one case in our survey of the first eleven years did the claimant specifically ask for punitive damages.[48] Not surprisingly, in this case the defendant's actions resulting in a *Charter* violation were also tortious. However, in several cases where the court awarded punitive damages, it is not clear whether they were awarded in the context of a civil wrong being committed or solely to punish the defendant for violating the plaintiff's *Charter* rights.[49] By contrast, there are examples of courts ex-

---

40 See Appendix 9.

41 See Appendix 10.

42 *Collin*, above note 14 (reversed on appeal); *BB*, above note 13; *Lord*, above note 13; *Patenaude*, above note 13.

43 *Crossman*, above note 13; *Freeman*, above note 14 (reversed on appeal); *F(RG)*, above note 13. Amounts awarded can be found in Appendix 10.

44 In *Rollinson*, above note 13, the Federal Court awarded the claimant $58,000 in aggravated damages, while the trial court in *Freeman*, above note 14, awarded $5,000 (reversed on appeal).

45 See cases listed at note 38, above in this chapter.

46 *Blouin*, above note 13.

47 *Lewis*, above note 13.

48 *Bauder*, above note 20.

49 See, for example, *Collin*, above note 14; *Freeman*, above note 14; *Lord*, above note 13.

plicitly declaring that punitive damages were being awarded to serve as a deterrent to potential future *Charter* violations.[50]

In all of these cases, the courts appear to assume, without discussion, that punitive or exemplary damages are a suitable remedy under section 24(1). The lack of discussion may be attributable to the fact that punitive damages are a well-recognized common law remedy designed to deter civil wrongs. If the judiciary accepts the fact that fundamental *Charter* rights are of more importance than ordinary common law rights and interests, then a well-recognized common law remedy like punitive damages should appropriately be used to deter potential *Charter* violations.[51]

8) Recurring Problems

a) Relationship between Sections 24(1) and 52(1) — The Problem of Concurrent Remedies

During the first evolutionary period, 1984–94, there were several problems that reoccurred and commanded judicial attention. One of these was the relationship between section 24(1) of the *Charter* and section 52(1) of the *Constitution Act, 1982*, which raised the issue of concurrent remedies. However, this seemed to be a non-issue for trial courts during this period because in several cases courts granted *Charter* remedies in the form of declarations of invalidity and *Charter* damages without any discussion of the problem of concurrent remedies.[52] This issue was specifically addressed by the Federal Court of Appeal in *Schachter* in 1990[53] and finally resolved by the Supreme Court of Canada in 1992.[54] There was no discussion of the problem of concurrent remedies by trial courts during the two-year period 1992 to 1994, the end of the first evolutionary period.

---

50 *F(RG)*, above note 13; *Rollinson*, above note 13; *Crossman*, above note 13; *BB*, above note 13.

51 The case of *Rollinson*, above note 13, is a good example. The concern about a court's awarding punitive damages arises from the fact that "they extract punishment without the safeguards of a criminal trial, they lead to multiple sanctions, they are difficult to assess and they provide the plaintiff with a windfall": Oonagh E Fitzgerald, *Understanding* Charter *Remedies: A Practitioner's Guide* (Scarborough, ON: Carswell, 1994) (loose-leaf 1994 revision) at 5-58.

52 *Blouin*, above note 13; *Crossman*, above note 13.

53 *Schachter* FCA, above note 9.

54 *Schachter* SCC, above note 8.

b) Tort Law Damages or Constitutional Damages or Both?

A second recurring problem involved the interface between the traditional common law remedy system for civil wrongs and the new provisions of the *Charter* for constitutional remedies. Money damages have traditionally been the primary civil remedy for tortious conduct involving individuals. If tortious conduct under the new *Charter* remedy regime also constitutes a constitutional tort, what should be the consequences? Should a court provide two remedies: one for the civil tort and another for the constitutional tort?

If the remedies requested were different, for example, one being money damages for any torts committed and the other a declaration of invalidity or a stay of proceedings as the *Charter* remedy, two remedies might be possible. But if the remedy requested by the claimant was (1) for money damages for the civil wrong or tort and (2) for money damages for the constitutional violation, what should be the result? Crown counsel inevitably raised the issue, and this led to a further question not always articulated by the courts, namely, are civil wrongs or torts and constitutional torts qualitatively different? If so, do they require different remedies?

There are several reasons why claimants might want to bring claims for *Charter* damages in addition to any other claims that they might put forth, usually in torts. Firstly, claimants might hope that they will not have to prove all the elements of a tort claim in their *Charter* action, even though it might be based on the same set of facts. Secondly, they might hope that the defence of qualified immunity, which is frequently raised as a defence by the Crown in a tort action, will not be applied by the court. Thirdly, a claimant might optimistically hope that a court will not only award tort damages but will also award *Charter* damages in addition, thereby providing the claimant with a higher total compensation. Finally, a hopeful claimant might speculate that statutory time limitations will not be applicable to a *Charter* claim.[55]

In cases where the claim was for both civil damages in torts and constitutional damages, courts took the view that since both claims arose out of a single act, only one claim for money damages should succeed to avoid duplication. Of the twenty-one cases in our first-period review sample, tortious conduct on the part of the state was a factor in nine cases (43 percent), thus raising the potential problem of double recovery.[56] The issue of a tort-

55 See Robert E Charney & Josh Hunter, "Tort Lite? — *Vancouver (City) v. Ward* and the Availability of Damages for *Charter* Infringements" (2011) 54 *Supreme Court Law Review* (2d) 393.

56 *Crossman*, above note 13; *Blouin*, above note 13; *BB*, above note 13; *Breen*, above note 22; *Charters*, above note 22; *Bauder*, above note 20; *Rollinson*, above note 13;

and-*Charter* conflict was explicitly recognized by the court in 23 percent of the rejection cases.[57] Given the significance of the problem, it is surprising that in only one case did the court raise the question whether *Charter* damages should be looked upon differently than civil damages or assessed at a higher or more substantial level.[58] And even in this case, the British Columbia Court of Appeal did not make it clear whether it saw a qualitative difference between *Charter* damages and civil damages. By giving primacy to tort damages in cases of remedial overlap, the courts might well be seen to have been sending a message, perhaps not intentionally, that violation of *Charter* rights on their own does not need or merit special judicial recognition in the form of a distinctive *Charter* damages award. A more likely explanation perhaps is that the courts were more familiar with tort damages awards and more comfortable assessing damages for civil wrongs than they were wading into the unchartered waters of *Charter* damages.

c) Qualified Immunity Defence

A third problem, and one that reoccurred almost as frequently, involved situations where a *Charter* violation was the result of government officials acting pursuant to what they believed was a valid statutory authorization or other legal authority that was later declared by the courts to be constitutionally invalid. In such cases, the government official acted in good faith, but constitutional rights were still infringed. The common law doctrine of colour of right or good faith provides a successful defence to a tort action or other civil action against government officials. The question was, should the same defence be available in cases of constitutional torts or wrongs? At common law, the claimant or plaintiff has to establish malice, bad faith, or abusive process to overcome the defence. Courts had to determine whether the same requirement or burden of proof would be appropriate in cases of *Charter* violations.

Academic commentary during the period under review suggested that the common law defence of qualified immunity (as it was described) should be applied to *Charter* violations.[59] The counter-argument was that if the

---

Freeman, above note 14; *Patenaude*, above note 13.

57 *Breen*, above note 22; *Bauder*, above note 20; *Charters*, above note 22.

58 *R v Hamil* (1984), 14 CCC (3d) 338 (BCCA), Esson JA. The question was not raised by the Federal Court Trial Division in *Rollinson*, above note 13, when it awarded the claimant both common law tort damages and *Charter* damages.

59 Professor Cooper-Stephenson, above note 31, advocates the adoption of the test of immunity put forth by the US Supreme Court in *Harlow v Fitzgerald*, which states that "officials performing discretionary functions are generally shielded from liability for civil damages insofar as their conduct does not

defence were applied, countless citizens whose *Charter* rights had been infringed would be denied a remedy. Offsetting this argument was the concern that it was unfair or unjust to award a remedy and declare a constitutional wrong committed in circumstances where public officials did act in good faith relying upon legislation or legal process that they thought to be valid. To take this position would require officials to predict whether the legislation under which they acted would later be struck down by the courts.

As previously noted, in seven of the twenty-one cases the courts required that malice, bad faith, or improper motive on the part of the defendant be established.[60] The defence of qualified immunity was raised by the defendant in nine cases but applied by the courts in only seven. The references of the courts to this mental element were a response thereto. Five of the nine cases involved situations where government officials had acted pursuant to statutory authority that they thought was constitutionally valid but that was later declared to be unconstitutional.[61] In the remaining four cases, a statute was not involved. Instead, these cases involved government officials who either exceeded their authority or acted improperly when implementing valid statutory or other legal rules or processes.[62] The immunity defence was equally effective in both situations. Trial courts seemed prepared not only to apply the traditional common law doctrine of immunity regarding invalid statutes to *Charter* cases but also to extend that doctrine to other non-statute situations where the only problem was the improper actions of a government official.[63]

---

violate clearly established statutory or constitutional rights of which a reasonable person would have known": 457 US 800 at 818 (1982) [*Harlow*]. Similarly, Professor Marilyn L Pilkington, in her seminal article "Damages as a Remedy for Infringement of the *Canadian Charter of Rights and Freedoms*" (1984) 62:4 *Canadian Bar Review* 517 at 576, declares that damages will not be available for a violation of the *Charter* if the government official acted in good faith and in reliance on the then current state of constitutional law. This is basically an expression of the *Harlow* test.

60 For a list of these cases, see Appendix 12.

61 *Scorpio Rising Software Inc v Saskatchewan* (AG) (1986), 46 Sask R 230 (QB); *Lewis*, above note 13; *S Bertram Miller*, above note 14; *Lagiorgia*, above note 19; *Crown Trust*, above note 14.

62 *McGillivray*, above note 14; *Lord*, above note 13; *Stenner*, above note 14; *Collin*, above note 14.

63 An alternate approach, suggested by Fitzgerald, above note 51 at 5-64, to the question of Crown immunity is to consider the issue of government conduct as an inquiry under s 32 of the *Charter*. In this approach, the question becomes whether the *Charter* applies to the particular actor's conduct rather than a remedial question. As Fitzgerald explains:

d) The Need for Actual or Real Injury or Loss

A related vexing question debated by the early courts was whether *Charter* violations had to result in actual damages of some sort or whether a violation *per se* was sufficient to support a money damages award. In common law, for some torts (not including negligence) mere violation of the protected civil right is sufficient to support a tort remedy, and no actual loss or damages need to be proven. However, in most of these torts, some degree of fault has to be either proven or disproven. Ultimately the question for the early courts was whether *Charter* rights were sufficiently important to warrant a money damages remedy when there were neither real nor actual damages and when there was no fault involved.

The overwhelming majority of cases in our early sample of twenty-one declared that fault was a requirement or that good faith was a defence or that damages *per se* could not be awarded. In only one case did a court award damages *per se*.[64] In fact, if the claimants had suffered no real injury or loss, courts were inclined to require a showing of not just ordinary fault but greater fault in the form of malice.[65]

9) Concluding Remarks

The first eleven years of judicial experience with section 24(1) of the *Charter*, specifically with reference to *Charter* damages as a remedy, show trial courts doing their best to come to grips with their newly acquired judicial discretion. Because courts were unsure of both how *Charter* damages differed from ordinary civil damages and how the two were intended to interact when a given government act constituted both a civil wrong and a constitutional violation, it is no wonder that their decisions lacked consistency. Without authoritative pronouncements from Canada's highest court to guide them as to the purpose or purposes of *Charter* damages, lower courts offered few extended explanations of their section 24(1) decisions or the

---

> [I]f the case falls with s.32, then one proceeds to the *Charter* analysis, first of a specific rights violation and secondly of the issue of justification under s.1. Once a *Charter* violation is established, the remedies question itself is not defined by immunity considerations but by the language of s.24(1) which calls for a remedy that is appropriate and just in the circumstances.

Early experience with the *Charter* and *Charter* claims indicates that this approach has not been used to address the issue of government immunities as a defence to a *Charter* claim for damages.

64 *Lord*, above note 13.

65 For a list of these cases, see Appendix 12.

rationale underlying the concept of *Charter* damages. The one consistent factor in these early decisions is the very cautious approach that courts of appeal took to the availability of *Charter* damages as a constitutional remedy.

Chapter 2

Supreme Court of Canada Decisions

1984–94

A. INTRODUCTION

Although lower courts of necessity had to make decisions about the availability of *Charter* damages as a remedy for *Charter* violations within a few years of the enactment of the *Canadian Charter of Rights and Freedoms* and section 24(1),[1] the Supreme Court of Canada did not make any kind of authoritative pronouncement on the issue until 1994.[2] The time lag is not surprising given the cost of appealing a case to Canada's highest court and the time it usually takes for any case to ascend the judicial ladder. When the case of *RJR – MacDonald Inc v Canada* (AG)[3] did reach the Supreme Court in 1994, the primary issue for the Court was *not* whether money compensation could be awarded as a remedy under section 24(1) but whether the Court could and should provide interlocutory relief to delay the legal effect of tobacco regulations that had been passed and to prevent public authorities from enforcing them. The interlocutory relief in question was a stay and an injunction.

The issue of *Charter* damages arose only incidentally as part of the judicial discussion of irreparable harm and the suitability of damages as an alternative remedy. Justices Sopinka and Cory, writing for the majority, suggested that the assessment of irreparable harm in an interlocutory application involving *Charter* rights would often be more difficult than a comparative assessment in a private law application.[4] One reason for such

1 Part I of the *Constitution Act, 1982*, being Schedule B to the *Canada Act 1982* (UK), 1982, c 11 [*Charter*].

2 *RJR – MacDonald Inc v Canada* (AG), [1994] 1 SCR 311 at 342 [*RJR – MacDonald*].

3 *Ibid.*

4 *Ibid* at 341.

difficulty, the Court suggested, is that the notion of irreparable harm is clearly tied to the remedy of damages, but, as the Court pointed out, they are *not* the primary remedy in *Charter* cases.[5] However, Sopinka and Cory JJ did declare that the Supreme Court had, in previous cases, accepted the principle that damages could be awarded for breach of *Charter* rights.[6]

The Court ultimately concluded that the plaintiff's request for a stay to delay the effect of the tobacco regulations should be denied. As a result, there was no need for the Court to consider the issue of injunctive relief or, in the alternative, a damages award. Nonetheless, the Supreme Court's comments about damages, whether considered observations or *obiter dicta*, remain part of the judicial record. In total, the Court offered three significant observations about *Charter* damages, two of which have already been mentioned: (1) *Charter* damages are not the primary remedy in *Charter* cases; (2) the Court had, on several prior occasions, accepted the principle that damages may be awarded for breach of *Charter* rights; and (3) there was a lack of developed *Charter* jurisprudence.[7] These observations although technically only *dicta* nevertheless provide objective evidence of the Court's thinking regarding *Charter* damages. As such, they offer important and much needed guidance for lower courts. They also warrant further detailed discussion.

B. OBSERVATION — DAMAGES MAY BE AWARDED FOR A *CHARTER* VIOLATION

I will deal with the Supreme Court of Canada's second observation first because it is the most fundamental. The Supreme Court noted that it had on several prior occasions accepted the principle that damages may be awarded for breach of *Charter* rights. This comment is not entirely accurate. There had been earlier cases, which preceded *RJR – MacDonald*,[8] in which individual members of the Court had made comments about the availability of damages as a section 24(1) remedy, but the Court as a whole had never collectively agreed with this opinion. It is true that in the case of *R v Mills*,[9] Lamer CJ, dissenting, had suggested that damages could possibly be awarded along with a stay of proceedings. However, this speculation was dependent upon proof of malice on the part of the Crown resulting in prejudice

5 *Ibid.*
6 *Ibid.*
7 *Ibid.*
8 *RJR – MacDonald*, above note 2.
9 [1986] 1 SCR 863 [*Mills*].

to the accused. Chief Justice Lamer repeated his opinion two years later in *R v Rahey*.[10] We should note that the main issue in both of these cases was whether the Court could award damages along with or concurrently with a stay of proceedings in a criminal action and not whether damages were an appropriate and just remedy *per se*. The issue raised in *Mills* and *Rahey* was put to rest by the Supreme Court in its decision in *Schachter v Canada* in 1992.[11]

Another comment by an individual Supreme Court justice was delivered by Wilson J, dissenting, in the case of *McKinney v University of Guelph*.[12] On this occasion, Wilson J remarked that it would be appropriate and just to award *Charter* damages as compensation for real harm if it flowed directly from the *Charter* violation.[13] Justice Wilson added that damages would generally be awarded unless compelling reasons dictated otherwise. Although a lone voice in the Court at this time, at least Wilson J was addressing the issue of *Charter* damages availability directly as the main issue.

One year before the *RJR – MacDonald* decision, McLachlin CJ writing for the Court and commenting upon the adequacy of a stay as a remedy had declared, "nor would I rule out other remedies such as damages."[14] Here again we have another indirect reference to damages as a remedy by an individual Supreme Court justice, and the assumption seems to be that they are available.

In the *RJR – MacDonald* case, Sopinka and Cory JJ did refer to comments by Lamer J in *Mills*, but no reference was made to the comments by Wilson J in *McKinney* or McLaughlin CJ in *R v Potvin*. They also referred to the Supreme Court's collective decision in *Nelles v Ontario*[15] to support their contention that in earlier cases the Court had accepted the principle that damages might be awarded as a *Charter* remedy. However, in *Nelles* the primary issue was not *Charter* damages but whether the common law defence of absolute prosecutorial immunity, which applied in non-*Charter* cases, would also apply to the *Charter*. If the defence applied, the discussion of remedies would be irrelevant. It was in this context that Lamer J, for himself and two other members of the Court, warned, "the existence of absolute immunity may bar a person whose *Charter* rights have been infringed from applying to a competent court for a just and appropriate remedy in the form

---

10 [1987] 1 SCR 588 [*Rahey*].

11 [1992] 2 SCR 679 [*Schachter*].

12 [1990] 3 SCR 229 [*McKinney*].

13 *Ibid* at 386. Note Wilson J's specific reference to "real harm."

14 *R v Potvin*, [1993] 2 SCR 880 at 897.

15 [1989] 2 SCR 170 [*Nelles*].

of damages."[16] Again the assumption seems to be that damages would be an appropriate remedy under section 24(1), but this issue was never directly raised or discussed by the Court. Reference to damages as a remedy was made but more as an example of a remedy that would be precluded if the absolute immunity defence were available. Perhaps the Supreme Court was just assuming that damages were appropriate and just as a *Charter* remedy, but it certainly did not discuss the issue directly. Overall, the evidence used by Sopinka and Cory to support their conclusion was not very substantial.

C. OBSERVATION — DAMAGES ARE NOT THE PRIMARY *CHARTER* REMEDY

The Supreme Court of Canada's first observation in *RJR – MacDonald*[17] that damages are not the primary remedy in *Charter* cases is based on the fact that when a law is challenged as being unconstitutional pursuant to section 52(1) of the *Constitution Act, 1982*,[18] the complainant usually requests a declaration of invalidity, a stay of proceedings, or both as the primary remedy. If damages were to be claimed as a remedy as well, the request would have to be made under section 24(1). The question that arises is whether a court could or should award concurrent remedies under sections 24(1) and 52(1).

The Supreme Court in *Schachter* declared that a remedy under section 24(1) would rarely be available concurrently with a declaration of unconstitutionality under section 52(1).[19] It did not rule out the possibility entirely but made it clear that the remedy of damages would not usually be granted along with a declaration of unconstitutionality. There appear to be two objections to a court's issuing concurrent remedies. Firstly, as already noted, the functions of the two sections are different even though both can involve providing remedies: section 52(1) decisions affect many people whereas section 24(1) decisions affect individual claimants. Secondly, awarding damages after a law is declared unconstitutional gives the remedy retroactive effect, a result that the courts are reluctant to produce.

Another complicating factor that may have contributed to the Supreme Court's view that damages were not a primary remedy is the fact that many of the early cases were criminal law cases. Judges had some difficulty providing a civil law remedy like damages in criminal proceedings. This concern was usually expressed in the context of the question whether or not

---

16 *Ibid* at 196.

17 *RJR – MacDonald*, above note 2.

18 Being Schedule B to the *Canada Act 1982* (UK), 1982, c 11.

19 *Schachter*, above note 11.

the court involved was a court of competent jurisdiction.[20] As La Forest J explained or chided, "civil remedies should await action in a civil court."[21] Given these considerations, it is not difficult to see why the Supreme Court made the observation it did regarding the non-primacy of the damages remedy.

Justice Wilson's comments and observations about damages as a *Charter* remedy in *McKinney*[22] treat damages as a more significant *Charter* remedy than do comments from other members of the Court. There may be several reasons for this. First of all, *McKinney* was not a criminal law case, and so the problem of a court's awarding civil damages in a criminal law proceeding was not an issue. Secondly, because the majority of the Court concluded that the *Charter* did not apply to a university, the problem of concurrent remedies did not arise either. Thus the two main factors that would relegate the damages remedy to a subordinate role were not present in *McKinney*. Finally, *McKinney* was the first case coming before the Supreme Court in which damages as a *Charter* remedy was specifically requested. Thus the context within which Wilson J had made her remarks about *Charter* damages was quite different from that in which Sopinka and Cory JJ made theirs in *RJR – MacDonald*. Because the majority in *McKinney* concluded that the *Charter* did not apply, there was no need for it to discuss the issues of violation or remedies. Justice Wilson, on the other hand, concluded that the *Charter* did apply and that there was a violation and hence the need to consider damages as a potential *Charter* remedy.

In addition to her dissenting conclusion that damages were an appropriate and just remedy under section 24(1) and would generally be awarded unless there were compelling reasons not to,[23] Wilson J made several other important comments about *Charter* damages in *McKinney*. She suggested for example that different considerations respecting appropriate remedial relief should apply when constitutional rights and freedoms, as opposed to common law rights, are at stake.[24] In this case, the common law rights she had in mind were contractual rights. This suggestion is clearly a warning that *Charter* damages are not the same qualitatively as common law damages. Just how they differ, however, was not made clear, but the implication is that they are of a higher order.

---

20 See, for example, *R v Big M Drug Mart Ltd*, [1985] 1 SCR 295; *Mills*, above note 9.

21 *Mills*, above note 9 at 971.

22 *McKinney*, above note 12. See text associated with note 13, above in this chapter.

23 *Ibid* at 410–11.

24 *Ibid* at 408–9.

In addition, Wilson J's remarks regarding the defence of good faith and the financial impact that a damages award would have on the university are worth noting (particularly by lower courts). She declared, "Impecuniosity and good faith are not a proper basis on which to deny an award of compensatory damages."[25] In this case, a finding that a mandatory retirement policy was unconstitutional would have affected not only the claimants in the action but other faculty members forced to retire as well. The resulting financial impact on the university could have been significant. Fortunately for the university, the damages issue did not have to be considered by the Court. As far as Wilson J's comments about good faith are concerned, they would become very relevant to the decisions of lower courts in the next twenty years, when lower courts would find themselves grappling with issues of fault and the qualified immunity defence with much greater frequency.

D. OBSERVATION — LACK OF A DEVELOPED JURISPRUDENCE

The Supreme Court of Canada's third observation in *RJR – MacDonald*[26] that there was a lack of developed jurisprudence in relation to *Charter* damages is fully supported by the data on lower-court decisions during the period 1984 to 1994.[27] Lack of consistency in results is apparent and reflects the lack of any principled basis for the various lower-court decisions. The emergence of particular problems or issues, such as the application of the pre-existing common law defence of qualified immunity, the more general issue of the need for some mental element as a prerequisite factor for the award of *Charter* damages, or the tort-and-*Charter* conflict with regard to damages awards, was not addressed by the Supreme Court's decision in *RJR – MacDonald*. These issues would have to be settled at a later date.

The relatively bland response of the Supreme Court in *RJR – MacDonald* to the issue of *Charter* damages as a remedy and the lack of any effort to explore underlying purposes or principles is not totally surprising given the fact that the Court was dealing with interlocutory relief not necessarily involving civil damages as an alternative remedy. Lower-court experience with *Charter* damages was still fairly limited, and lower courts had done little to explore the possible purposes, principles, and scope of this new *Charter* remedy.

---

25 *Ibid* at 411.

26 *RJR – MacDonald*, above note 2.

27 For a list of these cases, see Appendix 1.

The "observations" of the Supreme Court in *RJR – MacDonald* regarding damages as a *Charter* remedy, while useful by making it clear that this remedy was available under section 24(1), did little to clarify in what circumstances damages could and should be awarded. While it is to be recognized that *Charter* damages were not the main issue in *RJR – MacDonald*, some judicial direction beyond approving use of this remedy would have been helpful. Justice Wilson in *R v Gamble*[28] had directed lower courts to adopt a purposive approach to both the *Charter* as a whole and section 24(1) in particular. However, decisions at both the lower-court level and the Supreme Court level show little clear evidence of this approach up to 1994.[29] Given the relatively few cases in which the issue of *Charter* damages was squarely placed before the Supreme Court for decision and comment, it is not surprising that a comprehensive discussion of underlying principles, functions, and purposes was not provided up to 1994. In *RJR – MacDonald*, the Supreme Court had an opportunity to begin the process of explanation but elected merely to note that judicial discussion of the principles that might govern an award of damages under section 24(1) had not yet developed.

28 [1988] 2 SCR 595.

29 During the first eleven years of *Charter* damages cases, lower courts engaged in little, if any, discussion of the purposes of the *Charter* or s 24(1). Nor did they apart from one or two cases address the question whether and in what way *Charter* damages were qualitatively different from civil tort damages.

Chapter 3

The Second Period of Evolution

1995–2010

A. INTRODUCTION

The second chronological period under review covers the years 1995 to 2010 and includes both the trial and Court of Appeal decisions in *Ward v Vancouver (City)*.[1] The sample of fifty cases decided by the courts during this period comprises sixty-four court decisions, or forty-six trial decisions and eighteen court of appeal decisions.[2] Of the fifty cases, eight involve federal courts, comprising thirteen decisions.[3]

B. SUCCESS RATE

Damages under the *Canadian Charter of Rights and Freedoms*[4] were awarded by the courts in approximately one-third of the cases and rejected in two-thirds.[5] Looking only at court of appeal decisions, an almost even split is

1 2007 BCSC 3 [*Ward* SC], aff'd 2009 BCCA 23 [*Ward* CA], var'd (*sub nom Vancouver (City) v Ward*) 2010 SCC 27 [*Ward* SCC].

2 These decisions can be found in Appendix 1.

3 *Pack MJ Inc v Canada*, [1998] FCJ No 1922 (CA) [*Pack MJ*]; *Dulude v Canada* (1997), 138 FTR 301 (TD), rev'd [2000] 1 FC 545 (CA) [*Dulude*]; *Pearson v Canada*, 2006 FC 931, aff'd 2007 FCA 380, leave to appeal to SCC refused, [2008] SCCA No 299 [*Pearson*]; *Samimifar v Canada (Minister of Citizenship and Immigration)*, 2006 FC 1301, aff'd 2007 FCA 248; *Khalil v Canada*, 2007 FC 923, aff'd 2009 FCA 66 [*Khalil*].

4 Part I of the *Constitution Act, 1982*, being Schedule B to the *Canada Act 1982* (UK), 1982, c 11 [*Charter*].

5 For ease of reference, these cases are listed in appendices 15 & 14. The precise figures show judicial awards in 34 percent of the cases and a rejection of claims in 66 percent of the cases.

found between awards and rejections.[6] These results stand in sharp contrast to the first period (1984–94) results, which showed a rejection rate by courts of appeal of almost 100 percent.[7]

C. REASONS FOR REJECTION

The most prevalent reason for rejecting *Charter* damages claims was the courts' insistence upon some level of fault, usually in the form of *mala fides*, or malicious conduct on the Crown's part. These cases accounted for 67 percent of the rejection cases during the period under review.[8] The second-most prevalent reason for rejection was claimants' failure to prove a *Charter* violation (21 percent).[9] Together these two bases for rejection accounted for almost 90 percent of all rejections. Other less statistically significant reasons for rejection of damages claims included application of the rule in *Schachter v Canada*[10] (three cases),[11] conflict with tort recovery (two cases),[12]

---

6 Of the fourteen court of appeal decisions involved, *Charter* damages were awarded in six cases and denied in eight cases. For a list of these decisions, see Appendix 16.

7 During the first review period, 1984–94, courts of appeal rejected damages claims in six cases while awarding damages in only one case. See Chapter 1, Section C(1), above, and for a list of the cases involved, see Appendix 7. The Quebec Court of Appeal in *Patenaude v Roy* (1994), 23 DLR (4th) 78 [*Patenaude*], was the only court of appeal to award *Charter* damages during this earlier period.

8 For a list of these cases, see Appendix 14.

9 For ease of reference, these cases are listed in Appendix 18.

10 [1992] 2 SCR 679 [*Schachter*].

11 The rule was applied in *Shewfelt v Canada* (1997), 28 BCLR (3d) 340 (SC); *Pack MJ*, above note 3; *Chua v MNR*, [2001] 1 FC 641 (TD).

12 *Jane Doe v Toronto (Metropolitan) Commissioners of Police* (1998), 39 OR (3d) 487 (Gen Div) [*Jane Doe*]; *Ernst v Quinonez*, [2003] OTC 847 (SCJ) [*Ernst*].

application of a limitation period (one case),[13] and the availability of an alternative remedy (one case).[14]

D. AMOUNT OF AWARDS

In the second reporting period, damages awards ranged from a modest $500[15] to a very substantial $230,000.[16] This latter award is exceptional in that it reflects a serious *Charter* violation that resulted in the wrongful conviction and imprisonment of the claimant for a considerable length of time. The award reflects this tragic situation, but its size significantly inflates the average *Charter* award — being $26,739 — for the period 1995 to 2010. This average award is about one and a half times the average award received by claimants in the first eleven years of *Charter* experience and, at first glance, appears to reflect a more generous judicial approach. However, if the exceptional award of $230,000 is excluded, the average *Charter* damages award becomes $12,482. To obtain an accurate comparison of the second-period average award with the earlier period, the significant amount of $100,000 ordered by the Quebec Court of Appeal in the case of *Patenaude v Roy*[17] in the earlier period should be excluded from the calculations. When this is done, the average *Charter* damages award for the period 1984 to 1994 is similarly reduced to $4,785. A comparison of the average *Charter* award corrected to

13 *Pearson*, above note 3. The trial judge noted that the Supreme Court had not yet (as of 2006) ruled specifically on the question whether provincial limitation of actions statutes applied to the *Charter*. Such a ruling would come one year later in *Kingstreet Investments Ltd v New Brunswick (Finance)*, 2007 SCC 1 [*Kingstreet*], in which the Supreme Court held that s 9 of the *Limitation of Actions Act*, RSNB 1973, c L-8, applied to claims for personal *Charter* remedies. As McLachlin CJ explained two years later in *Ravndahl v Saskatchewan*, 2009 SCC 7, the *Kingstreet* decision held that "limitation periods apply to claims for personal remedies that flow from the striking of an unconstitutional statute" (*Kingstreet*, *ibid* at para 17). Provincial limitation statutes do not apply to *in rem* remedies granted pursuant to s 52(1) of the *Constitution Act, 1982*, being Schedule B to the *Canada Act 1982* (UK), 1982, c 11.

14 *Khalil*, above note 3.

15 *Chrispen v Prince Albert (City) Police Department* (1997), 148 DLR (4th) 720 (QB) [*Chrispen*].

16 *McTaggart v Ontario*, [2000] OTC 855 (SCJ) [*McTaggart*]. The trial court awarded the claimant a total of $230,000 in *Charter* damages, comprising $210,000 in general damages and $20,000 in punitive damages. This exceptionally high award was to compensate the claimant for six years of unlawful confinement.

17 *Patenaude*, above note 7.

exclude the two exceptional cases shows an increase in the average award of $7,697 for the period 1995 to 2010. This could be the result of a larger pool of data or a judiciary more informed about the role of *Charter* damages as a constitutional remedy.

E. *CHARTER* SECTIONS INVOLVED

Sections 7 and 8 of the *Charter* continue to be the most frequently violated sections and constitute the basis for half of the *Charter* damages claims in the fifteen years under review.[18] If section 9 is also included, the three sections together account for 61 percent of the separate claims.[19] This is slightly less than the 62 percent involvement rate for these sections in the first eleven years. Where we do see a difference is in the involvement rate of section 9 with more than a sixfold increase in cases over the first eleven years.[20] This is a significant increase even allowing for the longer period. Similarly, the number of cases involving section 15 showed a fivefold increase.[21]

F. FAULT REQUIREMENT

As previously indicated,[22] the requirement that the claimant prove some specific state of mind or faulty behaviour on the part of the defendant accounted for 67 percent of the damages claims rejections. In fifteen of the twenty-two cases involved, the courts required a high level of fault usually described as involving malice, bad faith, recklessness, or wilful disregard of *Charter* rights.[23] In only seven of the twenty-two cases did the courts concede that some degree of civil fault was sufficient to support a claim for

---

18 There were twenty alleged violations of s 7 and twelve alleged violations of s 8. Together, these two sections accounted for 43 percent of the total number of separate *Charter* claims in the cases under review. For a list of the cases involved, see Appendix 19.

19 There were thirteen cases involving s 9. For a list of these cases, see Appendix 20.

20 Going from two cases in the period 1984–94 to thirteen cases in the period 1995–2010.

21 Going from two cases in the period 1984–94 to ten cases in the period 1995–2010. For a complete list and breakdown of the *Charter* sections involved during the period 1995–2010, see Appendix 19.

22 See Section C, above in this chapter.

23 These cases are listed in Appendix 17.

Charter damages.[24] The defence of qualified immunity was raised in only two of the former fifteen cases[25] indicating that the very high standard of fault required by the courts in the other thirteen cases was not in response to the defence of qualified immunity put forth by the defendant. In the majority of these cases, the high standard of malice or bad faith was imposed upon the claimants with respect to government officials who were carrying out their functions under the authority of constitutionally valid, rather than invalid, statutes or laws. In other words, the liability bar for claimants was set at an equally high level for operational activities of government officials implementing valid laws. The requirement that the plaintiff prove malice or bad faith on the part of the government or its agents may have been influenced somewhat by the respondents' invocation of the qualified immunity defence in cases involving invalid statutes, but it is more likely that lower courts were simply applying the common law principles of public authority liability as put forth by the Supreme Court of Canada in the *Welbridge Holdings Ltd v Greater Winnipeg*[26] and *Central Canada Potash Co Ltd v Government of Saskatchewan*[27] cases.

G. TYPE OF DAMAGES AWARDED

Courts continued to award primarily compensatory damages during the second period under review.[28] Non-pecuniary damages in the form of anxiety, distress, loss of dignity, and humiliation were routinely mentioned as compensable consequences of *Charter* violations. The almost total absence of punitive damages as a separate head of damages was noticeable during the period 1995 to 2010.[29] Perhaps courts had built into the compensatory award a punitive component without specifically indicating this. In several cases courts awarded what they described as symbolic or moral damages.[30] A closer examination of these cases suggests that such labels essentially

24 *Ibid.*

25 *Pearson*, above note 3; *Trociuk v British Columbia (AG)*, 2008 BCSC 1597 [*Trociuk*].

26 [1971] SCR 957.

27 [1979] 1 SCR 42.

28 See Appendix 1.

29 Punitive damages were awarded in only one case: *McTaggart*, above note 16.

30 See, for example, *Dulude*, above note 3 (moral damages); *Auton (Guardian ad litem of) v British Columbia (Minister of Health)*, 2001 BCSC 220 [*Auton* SC], var'd 2002 BCCA 538 [*Auton* CA], rev'd 2004 SCC 78 (symbolic damages). However, in the case of *Trociuk*, above note 25, the British Columbia trial court refused to award symbolic damages.

cover what the civil law of tort damages would describe as aggravated damages, or perhaps they represent a vindication of *Charter* rights. In no case did the courts clearly declare that they were awarding *per se* damages. However, the damages award by the trial court in *Ward v Vancouver (City)*[31] could be described as *per se* damages, and it was, in fact, so labelled by Saunders JA dissenting in the Court of Appeal.[32]

H. RECURRING PROBLEMS — SOME OLD, SOME NEW

1) Some Old Problems

The issue of fault, either as a court-imposed prerequisite for a successful *Charter* damages claim or merely as one factor in the case, continued to be an active issue in the second period with a 19 percentage point increase in the percentage of cases in which it was a prerequisite and a 22 percentage point increase in the percentage of cases in which it was only one factor.[33] The tort-and-*Charter* conflict and overlap continued to be a live issue but in a decreasing number of cases.[34] The issue of the appropriateness of a global award was raised in one case.[35] The question whether the qualified immun-

---

31 *Ward*, above note 1.

32 *Ibid* at para 88.

33 In the present survey, fault is considered to be a factor in the court's decision if it was alleged by the claimant, discussed by the court, or specifically made a prerequisite to a damages award by the court. During the first period of the survey, 1984–94, fault was a factor in thirteen or 62 percent of the twenty-one cases. During the second period, 1995–2010, fault was found to be a factor in forty-two or 84 percent of the fifty cases. But if only those cases where fault was specifically required as a prerequisite by the courts are considered, the fault rate falls to 62 percent, compared to 43 percent for the first period.

34 It was the deciding factor in only two cases: *Jane Doe*, above note 12; *Ernst*, above note 12.

35 Courts use the term "global award" to describe the amount of compensation determined by a court to be appropriate when assessing personal injury damages in a civil tort action. It is the total amount of compensation arrived at by assessing separate and discrete heads of damages that reflect different types or aspects of personal injuries legally recognized by the courts as compensable. Rather than putting a dollar amount on each kind or type of damages, the court takes them all into account and arrives at a total, single corporate award or global award. Beside *Bevis v CTV Inc (cob ATV/CTV)*, 2004 NSSC 247 [*Bevis* SC], var'd 2006 NSCA 56 [*Bevis* CA], other cases such as *Dulude*, above note 3, and *Curry v Canada*, 2006 FC 63, also appear to be examples of courts making global awards though the awards were not described as such. The

ity defence applied to *Charter* cases continued to engage the attention of the Supreme Court of Canada.[36] Finally, the problem of how to present a *Charter* damages claim to a jury arose for the first time.[37]

During the period following 1994, two brave trial court judges valiantly tried to assess and summarize the developing jurisprudence of *Charter* remedies and damages. Justice Ducharme in *Hawley v Bapoo*[38] and Montigny J in *Pearson v Canada*[39] individually crafted comprehensive and thoughtful judgments tracing the development of section 24(1) jurisprudence and attempting a summary of the then current situation. Justice Ducharme, in particular, provided a very comprehensive survey of prior decisions in which *Charter* damages were claimed and either awarded or rejected. The courts in both *Bapoo* and *Pearson* came to some similar conclusions, a few of which reflect the earlier observations of the Supreme Court in the case of *RJR – MacDonald Inc v Canada (AG)*.[40] The conclusions of the two justices may be summarized as follows:

1) Damages, both compensatory and punitive, can be awarded if it is appropriate, and an action for any constitutional tort that may have been committed can be brought (*Bapoo*, *Pearson*, and *RJR – MacDonald*).
2) Damages are not the primary remedy (*RJR – MacDonald*), a fact that may account for the relatively few cases where they have been awarded. A second factor in the small number of successful cases is that many *Charter* damages actions are subsumed under tort actions (*Bapoo*).
3) There is an emerging consensus that section 24(1) provides, or is the basis for, independent relief in damages (*Pearson*).
4) It is not yet clear on what legal basis *Charter* damages rest. There has been no discussion of underlying principles by the courts (*Pearson* and *RJR – MacDonald*).
5) Caselaw has not been consistent with regard to whether or not there should be fault requirements and, if so, what the fault requirements should be (*Bapoo*).

Nova Scotia Court of Appeal in *Bevis* was critical of the trial judge's decision to limit the jury's assessment of damages to a global analysis of the overall physical experience of the claimants: *Bevis* CA, *ibid* at para 66.

36 *Guimond v Quebec (AG)*, [1996] 3 SCR 397 [*Guimond*]; *Mackin v New Brunswick (Minister of Finance)*, 2002 SCC 13 [*Mackin*].

37 *Bevis* CA, above note 35.

38 (2005), 76 OR (3d) 649 (SCJ), var'd 2007 ONCA 503 [*Bapoo*].

39 *Pearson*, above note 3.

40 [1994] 1 SCR 311 [*RJR – MacDonald*].

6) The role of malice in the *Mackin* type of situation where the qualified immunity defence is raised needs to be clarified (*Bapoo*). There is disagreement regarding the need for bad faith (*Pearson*).
7) With regard to *Charter* interpretation, a court should apply a generous rather than a legalistic interpretation. It should apply the principles outlined in *Doucet-Boudreau v Nova Scotia (Minister of Education)*[41] (*Bapoo* and *Pearson*).

Our study of cases decided during the period 1995 to 2010 supports and confirms these conclusions.

2) Some New Problems

a) Problems of Language and Definition — Moral and Symbolic Damages

To further complicate an already difficult and ambiguous situation, before the *Ward*[42] decision courts used a variety of descriptive terms when discussing or referring to *Charter* damages. Terms such as "symbolic" and "moral" were also used to describe what appear to be different kinds or types of *Charter* damages.[43] Survey results reveal that courts awarded compensation both in situations where the plaintiff suffered real tangible losses that would be compensable by a common law court and also in situations where the *Charter* violation did not result in any real or tangible harm. Most courts used the term "damages" to describe the money compensation awarded (if this was the case). One court, however, expressed the preference for the term "remedial compensation" rather than damages because the term was considered more consistent with the working of section 24(1).[44]

Standing on its own, the term "moral damages" could mean the same as "symbolic damages." In other words, the claimant suffered no actual legally recognized damages or loss, but in the court's opinion there was a need to emphasize or indicate the importance of the constitutional rights that

41 2003 SCC 62 at paras 53–58 [*Doucet-Boudreau*], Iacobucci and Arbour JJ for the court: these principles stress that any remedy provided by the court pursuant to s 24(1) as being "appropriate and just" should (1) vindicate *Charter* rights, (2) be legitimate within the framework of our constitutional democracy, and (3) be fair and just to the parties and not impose substantial hardships that are unrelated to securing the right.

42 *Ward*, above note 1.

43 As in *Dulude*, above note 3.

44 *Euteneier v Lee* (2003), 113 CRR (2d) 44 (Ont Div Ct), rev'g in part [2000] OTC 833 (SCJ), rev'd 2005 CanLII 33024 (Ont CA) [*Euteneier*].

had been infringed. It is possible that vindication may not be an element of moral damages and that they are awarded only to compensate intangible losses such as humiliation, embarrassment, or other emotional responses not legally recognized as injuries that qualify for compensation at common law.

The term "moral damages" was used by the Federal Court of Appeal in *Dulude v Canada*[45] to describe *Charter* damages in the amount of $10,000 awarded to a member of the Canadian armed forces for unlawful entry and detention. In this case, the court determined that the acts of the defendant had been non-intentional and non-malicious and caused no real or legally recognized harm. However, *Charter* rights had been infringed, and the court acknowledged that the plaintiff had suffered anxiety, anguish, and frustration in his attempt to validate his constitutional rights. The term "moral damages" as used in *Dulude* appears to be a civil law term used by Quebec courts to award the equivalent of common law aggravated damages.[46] However, there appears to be one significant difference in the basis for such damages. At common law, aggravated damages are awarded when (1) the defendant's conduct is unusually nasty or egregious and when (2) this has the effect of increasing the emotional trauma suffered by the victim.[47] Both elements have to be present. In the Quebec concept of *damages morale*, only the latter element (emotional trauma) appears to be required. Nasty or egregious conduct is reflected in an award for punitive damages. In *Dulude*, the court refused to award punitive damages because the conduct was not malicious.

The $20,000 in symbolic damages awarded to each claimant in *Auton (Guardian ad litem of) v British Columbia (Minister of Health)*[48] by the trial judge was intended "to advance the twin remedial purposes of governmental behaviour modification and compensation." As Allan J explained, the "award provides partial, albeit minimal, compensation to the petitioners and acknowledges the intransigence of Government in responding to long-standing requests and demands for autism treatment."[49] The claimants in *Auton* alleged that the government had failed to provide effective autism

---

45 Above note 3 at para 18.

46 See, for example, *Beliveau St Jacques v FRESP*, [1996] 2 SCR 345 [*Beliveau*]. In this case, the Court was considering s 49 of the Quebec *Charter of Human Rights and Freedoms*, RSQ 1975, c C-12 [Quebec *Charter*], which uses the phrase "moral or material prejudice" when discussing damages.

47 For a more complete discussion and explanation of the nature of aggravated damages at common law, see Kenneth D Cooper-Stephenson & Iwan B Saunders, *Personal Injury Damages in Canada* (Toronto: Carswell, 1981) at 55–58.

48 *Auton* SC, above note 30.

49 *Ibid* at para 64.

treatment. Part of the claim, in addition to a request for a declaration, was for compensation to cover the cost to each claimant of past autism treatment. Justice Allan refused to compensate the claimants for all of their past expenses explaining that a just and appropriate award could not be determined by reference to the claimants' outlay of funds. It would therefore appear that the $20,000 in symbolic damages awarded to each claimant represented an amalgam of three ingredients including (1) some compensation for past expenses, (2) some damages to influence the government to change its policy and provide more extensive and effective autism treatment (government behaviour modification), and 3) perhaps some compensation for the frustration suffered by the claimants during the long period of government inaction. Some observers might consider the attempt to influence government policy an improper use of the judicial discretion embedded in section 24(1).

The British Columbia Court of Appeal confirmed the award.[50] However, one member found the terms "symbolic" and "moral" too vague, indicating a lack of definitive criteria for the assessment of the quantum of damages. Another member of the court suggested that while it might be possible to develop a coherent set of principles with regard to an award of symbolic damages as a *Charter* remedy, no such set of principles had yet been developed, and he declined the challenge to attempt to do so.[51] The case was appealed to Canada's highest court, and the award overturned on the basis that a *Charter* violation had not been proven.[52] The Supreme Court did not comment upon the lower courts' use of terms like "symbolic" or "moral" to describe *Charter* damages.

Four years later, the British Columbia Supreme Court in *Trociuk v British Columbia (AG)*[53] declined to award symbolic damages because, as the court explained, there was no need to advance the purpose of government behaviour modification.[54] The government in this case had acted quickly to amend offending legislation, unlike the *Auton* case. Vindication as one element in a *Charter* damages award was not discussed in either *Auton* or *Trociuk*.

It is also possible that one component or element of a symbolic or moral damages award might be based upon a human rights type of injury to human dignity. At common law this type of affront is normally covered by an award

---

50 *Auton* CA, above note 30.

51 Justice Saunders thought that the terms were too vague (*ibid* at 452) while Lambert J declined the challenge (*ibid* at 463).

52 2004 SCC 78.

53 Above note 25.

54 *Ibid* at para 38.

of aggravated damages resulting from tortious acts. At least one court made such a reference when justifying a *Charter* damages award of $500.[55] An affront to dignity was also a factor in the *Dulude* case.[56] However, it is relevant to note that the Supreme Court in *Blencoe v British Columbia (Human Rights Commission)*[57] made it clear that human dignity is not an autonomous *Charter* right but may be a relevant consideration in determining what should be a just and appropriate quantum when awarding *Charter* damages.

Finally, one note on the use of the term "constitutional tort,"[58] which implies the need for or existence of some element of fault in the defendant's conduct that produced the *Charter* violation. Symbolic damages to the extent that vindication is an element in such an award do not necessarily involve fault. Moral damages, on the other hand, were declared by Gonthier J in *Guimond v Quebec (AG)*[59] to require malice or bad faith. The cases under review provide clear evidence of a need for more consistency in the use of terminology and a better understanding of the nature and purposes of *Charter* damages.

b) Tort-and-*Charter* Conflict — One System or Two?

As previously discussed, the problem of double recovery resulting from a tort-and-*Charter* claim overlap caused the rejection of 23 percent of the rejected *Charter* damages claims in the first review period.[60] During the recent longer period, the number of *Charter* damages claims rejected for the same reason fell to 6 percent of rejected claims.[61] Although showing a dramatic drop in occurrence, the problem of the relationship between a claim for a private law remedy in the form of compensation and a concurrent claim for

55 See *Chrispen*, above note 15 at 733.

56 Above note 45 at para 18.

57 2000 SCC 44.

58 This term was used to describe the nature of a *Charter* violation in several cases including *Crossman v Canada*, [1984] 1 FC 681 (TD); *McTaggart*, above note 16; *Pinnock v Ontario*, [2001] OJ No 2921 (SCJ); *Ferri v Ontario (AG)*, [2006] OJ No 710 (SCJ), var'd 2007 ONCA 79. Allen M Linden has expressed a preference "to classify these new civil actions for *Charter* violations as 'constitutional torts'" because so doing would "maintain a link to the fully developed field of tort law which would give some stability and guidance to judges administering this new area, while recognizing its public nature": "*Charter* Damage Claims: New Dawn or Mirage?" (2012) 39:4 *Advocates' Quarterly* 426 at 430.

59 *Guimond*, above note 36.

60 See Chapter 1, Sections C(2) and C(8)(b).

61 This represents two cases out of thirty-three: *Jane Doe*, above note 12; *Ernst*, above note 12.

a public law remedy of the same type continued to exist. The fact that two separate and distinct causes of action based upon a single set of circumstances gave rise to only one head of damages continued to be a problem for both common law and Quebec courts.

The problem is clearly illustrated by the 1998 case of *Jane Doe v Toronto (Metropolitan) Commissioners of Police*.[62] In this case, it was alleged that the rape of the plaintiff caused in part by the negligence of the local police force supported both a cause of action in negligence for failure to warn and a cause of action for breach of her constitutional rights under sections 7 and 15 of the *Charter*. As the court stated:

> [T]he plaintiff's damages are the same in respect of the two bases upon which her action is founded, i.e., negligence and breach of *Charter* rights . . . . In such circumstances the plaintiff is entitled to one award of damages to compensate her for the damage she has suffered. She is not, in my view, in these circumstances, entitled to any additional or "extra" damages because the police conduct has breached her *Charter* rights.[63]

The court did not say that Jane Doe was not entitled to a remedy for violation of her *Charter* rights but that her remedy would be limited to a declaration. Clearly the main emphasis for the court was compensation of the victim for her injuries suffered rather than vindication of *Charter* rights, which was not even mentioned by the court. The *Jane Doe* decision was decided prior to the Supreme Court of Canada decision in *Doucet-Boudreau*,[64] so vindication as a factor in *Charter* damages was not in the forefront of the trial judge's mind.

c) The Quebec Contribution

The one head of damages approach appeared to receive the approval of the Supreme Court of Canada in 1996 when Canada's highest court considered the issue of double compensation in a Quebec case involving the Quebec *Charter of Human Rights and Freedoms*.[65] In *Beliveau St Jacques v FRESP*,[66] the issue was whether the victim of an industrial accident in Quebec who had

---

62 *Jane Doe*, above note 12.

63 *Ibid* at 527.

64 *Doucet-Boudreau*, above note 41. In this case, the Supreme Court declared that vindication of *Charter* rights was one of the four characteristics of an appropriate and just remedy. See also note 41, above in this chapter.

65 Above note 46.

66 *Ibid.*

already received compensation under a provincial labour statute could also bring an action for compensation under section 49 of the Quebec *Charter*. Justice Gonthier speaking for the majority declared that "the [Quebec] *Charter* cannot authorize double compensation or be a basis for awarding damages separate from those that could have been obtained under the general law."[67] Justice Gonthier further stated, "The [Quebec] *Charter* does not create a parallel compensation system."[68]

Counsel for the plaintiff had argued in this case that the Quebec *Charter* had a formal autonomy that distinguished it from the general law of liability and that this fact was sufficient to characterize the remedy provided by section 49 as an original one. It was this argument to which the Supreme Court via Gonthier J was responding. The Court acknowledged the quasi-constitutional status of the Quebec *Charter* but noted that article 1053 of the *Civil Code of Quebec* reflects the principle that there is a judicial responsibility or obligation to repair damages done to others and that this same article provides the basis for liability for a violation of the same fundamental rights now protected by the Quebec *Charter*, such as freedom of conscience or religion.[69] Justice Gonthier further noted that the violation of a right protected by the Quebec *Charter* is equivalent to a civil fault, and by providing for exemplary damages, section 49 reinforces the parallel with civil liability.[70] What Gonthier J appears to be saying is that the Quebec *Charter* is a mere reflection of civil law principles, both with regard to rights and with regard to compensation remedies. And apparently a mere reflection is not sufficient evidence of an intention to create a parallel or separate compensation system that could include rules of procedure, rules of evidence, and its own jurisdiction.

It is also relevant to note that Gonthier J recognized that the Quebec *Charter* formalizes standards of conduct that apply to all individuals and in this sense falls into the category of public law but that he drew no distinction between public law and private law.[71] Nor did Gonthier J appear to consider the rights and freedoms set out in the Quebec *Charter* to be of an elevated status or different in any way from those of article 1053 of the *Civil Code of Quebec*. However, the Court described the Quebec *Charter* as a quasi-constitutional document,[72] which seems to indicate that it ranks lower on

67 *Ibid* at para 121.
68 *Ibid*.
69 *Ibid* at 405.
70 *Ibid*.
71 *Ibid*.
72 *Ibid* at 402.

the sanctity scale than the *Canadian Charter of Rights and Freedoms* but still represents a legal document of greater status than the *Civil Code of Quebec.*

In the same year that the *Beliveau* case was decided (1996), Gonthier J in another Quebec case, *Guimond*,[73] suggested that with the enactment of the *Canadian Charter of Rights and Freedoms*, the plaintiff is not limited to an action for damages under the general law of civil liability but could, in theory, seek compensation and punitive damages as an appropriate and just remedy under section 24(1) of the *Charter*.[74] This sounds very much like a recognition of a parallel system and appears to be at odds with the Court's earlier declaration in *Beliveau*. Perhaps the justices of the Supreme Court saw the *Canadian Charter of Rights and Freedoms* as having full or complete constitutional status or authority and therefore being superior to and more than a mere reflection of the common law or Quebec civil law. If so, this would indicate a clear recognition that a citizen whose *Charter* rights have been violated by the tortious act of another person has two different avenues available by which to seek compensation. However, the problem of double recovery would still be an issue.

d) The Dilemma of Common Law Courts

For common law courts, several questions arose as a result of these decisions. Firstly, what weight should a common law court give to the approach taken by the Supreme Court in cases involving the Quebec *Charter of Human Rights and Freedoms*?[75] Could it be considered completely analogous to the *Canadian Charter of Rights and Freedoms*?[76] Secondly, there appeared to be a difference in the approach taken by Gonthier J in the two cases. Which approach was the more authoritative?

In 2003, the Ontario Divisional Court in *Euteneier v Lee*[77] appeared to adopt the position posited by Gonthier J in *Guimond*[78] when it declared that a failure to approve one or more tort claims based on the same set of facts does not necessarily mean that a claim based on section 24(1) must fail. The court explained as follows:

> We do not doubt that cases will arise in which the decision to dismiss a tort claim will result in findings which are relevant to, and may be dis-

---

73 *Guimond*, above note 36.
74 *Ibid* at para 15.
75 Quebec *Charter*, above note 46.
76 *Charter*, above note 2.
77 *Euteneier*, above note 44.
78 *Guimond*, above note 36.

> positive of either a claim that Charter rights and freedoms have been breached or a claim for remedial compensation pursuant to s. 24(1).[79]

However, the Divisional Court continued, the court should consider the criteria for *Charter* damages separately from the criteria that govern an award of damages under the common law because the criteria covering common law and equitable rights and remedies do not necessarily limit section 24(1) of the *Charter*.[80]

Thus the Ontario Divisional Court clearly sees a difference between the basis of a common law tort claim and a *Charter* damages claim. Whether the parallel system of *Beliveau St Jacques v FRESP*,[81] rejected by Gonthier J, equates with different liability bases is unclear, but perhaps a parallel system involves more than just the bases for liability. Justice de Montigny clearly thought so in *Pearson* when he declared that

> there is a clear consensus [in the caselaw] that an award of damages contingent on a Charter violation must take place within the general legal regime of the province where the cause of action (or the alleged violation of a fundamental right) has taken place. This is to say that the rules governing evidence, procedure and jurisdiction related to this field of the law must generally find application, since the Charter itself does not provide a parallel architecture to that found in the various provincial and federal statutory schemes.[82]

e) Jury Trials — *Bevis v CTV Inc*

Three years after the Ontario Divisional Court decision in *Euteneier*,[83] the Nova Scotia Court of Appeal in *Bevis*[84] faced the same issue: the relationship between the common law remedial system and the remedies provided by

---

79 *Euteneier*, above note 44 at para 34.

80 *Ibid*.

81 *Beliveau*, above note 46.

82 *Pearson*, above note 3 at para 50. The issue of parallel jurisdiction arose in the *Pearson* case because the Crown (defendant) had argued that the plaintiff's claim for *Charter* damages had lapsed as a result of the time limitation in the *Civil Code of Québec*. Relying on *Beliveau*, above note 46 at para 44, the Crown had argued that a *Charter* damages claim should be treated as a civil claim and therefore subject to provincial statutes or provisions. Justice de Montigny agreed, noting that this was "indeed the position followed by most courts of the country with respect to time limitations related to claims for damages resulting from a violation of a Charter right" (*Pearson*, above note 3 at para 51).

83 *Euteneier*, above note 44.

84 *Bevis* CA, above note 35.

the *Charter*. This Nova Scotia case is of particular interest and importance for a couple of reasons. In addition to the continuing tort-and-*Charter* conflict in *Bevis*, the issue of *Charter* damages fell to be determined by a jury rather than a single judge.[85] The jury awarded general damages for wrongful search and seizure, and arbitrary and unlawful detention. The police officers involved had admitted liability to the claims, leaving the jury with only the question of the quantum of damages to be determined.

At trial, plaintiffs' counsel argued that damages should be calculated in terms of general damages plus aggravation for the intentional torts committed by the police officers with a second, separate award for general and aggravated damages for *Charter* violations. Defendant's counsel opposed such a division. After listening to the trial judge's instructions, the jury awarded each of the two claimants the sum of $1,500 general damages but declined to award aggravated damages. The claimants appealed on the following grounds:

1) The jury should have been instructed to consider *Charter* violations as separate and distinct heads of damages (which they did not do).
2) The trial judge failed to instruct the jury to consider the alleged violation of section 10(b) of the *Charter* (the right to retain counsel).
3) The trial judge was in error instructing the jury on the issue of aggravated damages when he found that the police officers had made a mistake stopping and detaining the plaintiffs but that they had exhibited no bad faith in doing so. Given the nature and number of the *Charter* offences committed, it was not open to the defendants to claim an innocent mistake.[86]

Speaking for the Nova Scotia Court of Appeal, MacDonald CJ allowed the appeal and directed a new hearing on the basis that, given the nature of the trial judge's instructions, the jury had been unable to fully appreciate the significance of the *Charter* rights that had been breached. It was the opinion of the Court of Appeal that omissions regarding section 24(1) had been significant enough to constitute an error of law.[87] More specifically,

---

85 Linden, above note 58 at 438, notes that jury trials may be available in the United States to hear constitutional tort cases. Section 24(1) makes no specific provision for *Charter* damages claims to be heard by a jury, but neither does the section specifically prohibit the use of jury trials. In those cases where a tort action might be heard by a jury in Canada, as was the case in *Bevis*, the constitutional issue can arise and will have to be addressed by a Canadian jury.

86 *Bevis* CA, above note 35 at para 17.

87 *Ibid* at para 65.

the jury had not been adequately instructed as to the importance of *Charter* rights in society, nor had they been instructed in assessing what would constitute an "appropriate and just" remedy in the event of a *Charter* breach. These omissions, declared the Court of Appeal, resulted in the jury being left with an inadequate appreciation of the potential significance of *Charter* breaches. This lack of appreciation affected the jury's decision to deny an award for aggravated damages.[88]

The main issue and argument at trial had focused on the question whether the plaintiffs' two-pronged claim for damages, one prong based on the intentional torts committed and the second based on violations of *Charter* rights, was sustainable in law. The defendant had argued that each plaintiff should be entitled to only one general damages award designed to compensate him for all the impugned conduct.[89] The trial judge stressed the need to avoid double recovery and recognized the *Charter* breaches as distinct sources of liability but was of the view that they should not constitute separate heads of damages. Instead, he declared, there should be one award arrived at by way of global analysis of all the misconduct.[90]

The Court of Appeal acknowledged the need to prevent double recovery, noting the Supreme Court of Canada decision in *Beliveau*,[91] which had rejected a separate stand-alone scheme for recovery of damages under the Quebec *Charter*. After raising the question whether the *Beliveau* approach should also apply to the Canadian *Charter* and noting the fact that the Supreme Court had yet to rule on this issue, MacDonald CJ stated that he was not prepared to "direct a new hearing simply because the [trial] judge refused to direct separate general damage awards under *s. 24(1)*."[92] As a result, the tort-and-*Charter* conflict and the issue of parallel systems remained unresolved. However, problems arising from a jury trial remained, in particular, the importance of the trial judge's instructions to the jury in a *Charter* damages claim.

In a jury trial, whether involving *Charter* damages or common law damages or both, the judge has a duty to instruct the jury as to the legal bases for awarding damages as well as how the quantum is to be determined. In *Bevis*, the trial judge did not read the precise wording of section 24(1) to the jury but instead told the jury that the *Charter* allows the court (the jury) to

---

88 *Ibid* at para 84.

89 *Ibid* at para 14.

90 *Bevis* SC, above note 35 at paras 5–8.

91 *Beliveau*, above note 46.

92 *Bevis* CA, above note 35 at para 61.

award damages when constitutional rights are infringed.[93] As to the applicable law, Moir J in his charge to the jury advised:

1) *Charter* violations constitute distinct sources of liability separate and apart from other civil wrongs.
2) They should not form separate heads of damages.
3) There is a need to avoid double recovery with regard to tort and *Charter* damages.
4) The jury should conduct a global analysis of the police conduct with a view to arriving at one award for general damages and one for aggravated damages, if appropriate.[94]

Justice Moir also refused to leave a possible violation of section 10 to the jury, explaining that any possible breach of the section would have no significant effect or impact on the quantum of damages.[95] The Court of Appeal disagreed, pointing out that in some cases courts had directed a modest damages award when this occurred.[96]

With regard to the appropriateness of a global award, MacDonald CJ expressed the view that it might have been appropriate for the jury to be properly instructed on the importance of *Charter* rights to every Canadian and the seriousness of any breach.[97] He further declared that it was not enough to simply add *Charter* violations to the mix with other common law torts without further elaboration.[98]

These remarks by MacDonald CJ require a jury (or judge) to specifically address *Charter* rights and their breach when issuing a global award, but it is not clear whether the actual amount awarded for *Charter* violations would also have to be specified. Comments made by MacDonald CJ later in his decision to the effect that had the only issue been the trial judge's refusal to direct separate damages awards for the civil wrongs committed (the torts) and the *Charter* violations, he would not have ordered a new trial, suggest that the actual amount awarded for *Charter* violations would not have to be specified.[99] The failure by the trial judge to provide the required relevant

---

93 See *ibid* at para 22, citing para 7 of Moir J's charge to the jury.
94 *Bevis* SC, above note 35 at paras 5–10.
95 *Ibid* at para 9.
96 *Bevis* CA, above note 35 at para 70.
97 *Ibid* at para 3.
98 *Ibid.*
99 *Ibid* at para 61.

instructions did, however, constitute misdirection significant enough to warrant a new hearing.[100]

Although not one of the grounds of appeal, MacDonald CJ observed that the omission in the pleadings of any claim for punitive damages was significant because it restricted the jury to awarding general damages.[101] In other words, it prevented the jury from awarding damages to deter further violations of *Charter* rights. Chief Justice MacDonald was of the view that the plaintiffs sought awards that would in essence punish the state for the *Charter* breaches but that, unfortunately, the plaintiffs had abandoned their claim for exemplary or punitive damages. He further observed that if the plaintiffs had made a blanket claim for relief under section 24(1), this would have given the jury the discretion to award punitive damages if they had considered this to be an appropriate remedy in light of the circumstances. As it was, they were limited to awarding compensatory damages for non-pecuniary losses. The jury were restricted to a consideration of conventional heads of damages, which would include aggravated damages.

i) Court of Appeal Suggestions for a Charge to the Jury

The fact that a number of laypersons rather than a single judge (at trial) would have the difficult task of determining what amount of compensation should be awarded to the plaintiffs meant that instructions by the trial judge in *Bevis* would have to be detailed enough to provide guidance.[102] The Court of Appeal suggested, in general, that the jury should be told precisely which *Charter* right had been violated by the conduct of the defendant and that the relevant sections of the *Charter* be read to the jury.

In addition, the purpose of the *Charter* should be explained, as Dickson J did in *Hunter v Southam Inc*[103] and *R v Big M Drug Mart Ltd.*[104] Following this, the trial judge should read to the jury the text of section 24(1) and have the jury provided with a copy of the section. With a copy in front of them, the jury should then be instructed as to the meaning of "appropriate and just," following the Supreme Court of Canada's explanation in *Doucet-Boudreau.*[105] Finally, the jury should be instructed as to the meaning of "meaningful vindication" and told to consider whether an enhanced general damages award would meaningfully affirm the *Charter* rights that had been violated

100 *Ibid* at para 68.
101 *Ibid* at para 46.
102 *Ibid* at para 64.
103 [1984] 2 SCR 145 at 161.
104 [1985] 1 SCR 295 at 344.
105 *Doucet-Boudreau,* above note 41.

in the case before them.[106] Moreover, in cases where section 24(1) has been claimed or invoked in conjunction with a claim for compensation based on an intentional tort, the jury should be instructed that section 24(1) cannot be considered in isolation.[107] With more specific reference to the case under consideration, the Court of Appeal stated that the jury should have been made aware of how the pleadings restricted the jury's discretion in awarding damages.[108]

These are all valid considerations that a trial judge would most likely have in mind when sitting without a jury and making a decision on a question of *Charter* damages. They were not included in the directions given to the jury by the trail judge in the *Bevis* case.

Unlike cases involving serious personal injuries, where an amount of $100,000 plus inflation has been established by the Supreme Court as a cap for non-pecuniary damages, no such cap has been developed for *Charter* damages.[109] As far as guidance for the jury is concerned in serious personal injury cases, the prevailing judicial opinion seems to be that the trial judge should make the jury aware of the upper limit or cap, particularly in cases where the judge thinks that the jury may award more than $100,000 plus inflation. In cases involving less serious injury, the civil procedure rules in several provinces allow trial judges to provide the jury with guidance in the form of a range of awards for different types of personal injuries.[110]

ii) **Charter *Violations and Aggravated Damages***

In the *Bevis* case, the plaintiffs claimed general damages and aggravated damages for both tort wrongs and *Charter* violations.[111] The trial judge

106 For an outline of suggested jury instructions, see *Bevis* CA, above note 35 at para 64.

107 *Ibid* at para 44.

108 *Ibid.*

109 In 1978, the Supreme Court decided three cases, all involving severely disabled plaintiffs: *Andrews v Grand & Toy Alberta Ltd*, [1978] 2 SCR 229 [*Andrews*]; *Thornton v School Dist No 57 (Prince George)*, [1978] 2 SCR 267; *Arnold v Teno*, [1978] 2 SCR 287. The Court in *Andrews*, *ibid* at 265, Dickson J, declared that $100,000 was the upper limit of non-pecuniary losses in cases of natural, i.e., catastrophic, injuries. For a fuller discussion of the trilogy and issues surrounding the new cap, see William HR Charles, *Charles Handbook on Assessment of Damages in Personal Injury Cases*, 2d ed (Toronto: Carswell, 1990) at 73ff.

110 See Linda D Rainaldi, ed, *Remedies in Tort* (Toronto: Carswell, 1987) (looseleaf 2014 supplement) vol 4, § 48.1 at 27-1105.

111 *Bevis*, above note 35. The claim for aggravated damages had initially been made in an action for defamation against the defendant CTV Inc: see *Bevis*

instructed the jury that the officers had merely made a mistake that had caused the *Charter* violation and that there was no evidence of bad faith.[112] Therefore, he suggested that aggravated damages would not be appropriate. And because the pleadings had ruled out any claim for punitive or exemplary damages, the only basis upon which an enhanced award to affirm or vindicate *Charter* rights could be made was via aggravated damages, or at least this is what the Court of Appeal seems to suggest.[113] A review of the cases examined here reveals that aggravated damages were claimed in several situations before *Bevis* but awarded for *Charter* violations in only one case.[114] In this case, the $5,000 awarded was described as being for both aggravated and punitive damages.[115]

In *Rollinson v Canada*,[116] the court awarded $58,400 in aggravated damages as part of general damages for torts that had been committed. A separate award of $8,000 was designated as *Charter* damages. In cases where aggravated damages had been claimed but were not awarded, this was because the evidence did not show malice, bad faith, or intentional disregard by the defendant of the plaintiff's *Charter* rights.[117] It is relevant to note that MacDonald CJ in *Bevis* expressed the view that a finding of bad faith might not be sufficient to establish an entitlement to aggravated damages in a *Charter* case.[118]

If we consider for a moment the rationale or basis for aggravated damages in tort claims, we find that they are awarded to provide solace to a plaintiff where the plaintiff's feelings have been wounded by the quality of

---

and Karela v CTV Inc, Burns and Kelly, 2004 NSSC 246. The issue of malice was raised as part of the defence.

112 See *Bevis* CA, above note 35 at paras 73 and 77, where MacDonald CJ referred to the instructions of the trial judge, Moir J.

113 See *ibid* at para 61.

114 Aggravated damages were claimed in *Lord v Allison* (1986), 3 BCLR (2d) 300 (SC) [*Allison*]; *Freeman v West Vancouver (District)*, 1991 CanLII 2365 (BCSC) [*Freeman* SC]; (1992), 19 BCAC 81 (CA), leave to appeal to SCC refused with costs (1993), 77 BCLR (2d) xxxi; *Morin v Prince Edward Island Regional Administrative Unit #3 School Board*, 2004 PESCTD 1, var'd 2005 PESCAD 14 [*Morin*]; *Ilnicki v MacLeod*, 2003 ABQB 465 [*Ilnicki*]. The court awarded aggravated damages in *Freeman* SC, *ibid*.

115 In *Freeman* SC, above note 114, the trial judge explained that "the nomenclature is of no real legal significance." Aggravated damages were awarded by the court in this case because the municipality refused to apologize for the unlawful detention of the claimant.

116 [1991] 3 FC 70 (TD); (1994), 20 CCLT (2d) 92 (FCTD).

117 See *Allison*, above note 114; *Morin*, above note 114; *Ilnicki*, above note 114.

118 *Bevis* CA, above note 35 at para 82.

the defendant's behaviour. Aggravated damages, in essence, constitute a balm for mental distress, that is, distress in the form of humiliation, indignation, outrage, or fear of repetition. These elements of emotional distress are a variety of non-pecuniary damages that are caused by the defendant's high-handed manner. The theory is that the plaintiff's sense of injury, in the sense of any emotional response to the wrongful act, is significantly heightened.

Aggravated damages are usually awarded in cases of intentional wrongdoing, but they can also be awarded in negligence actions where the plaintiff's emotional trauma is increased by the defendant's extreme recklessness.[119] The distress need not flow from any personal injury. At common law, for aggravated damages to be awarded by the court there must be proof of some egregious conduct on the part of the defendant and heightened trauma or response on the part of the plaintiff.

In the case of *Charter* violations that are accompanied by tortious acts, aggravated damages might be warranted depending upon the egregious nature of the defendant's acts. However, the survey data shows few cases where the courts have actually awarded aggravated damages in these circumstances.[120] In cases where the plaintiff's dignity has been affected or where some other fairly serious emotional response has been caused, it is very likely that, instead of awarding aggravated damages as a separate head of damages, the courts have merely increased the compensatory general damages to take into account the heightened emotional response. But in a given situation if the tortious acts are not serious or if there are none, is there any room or place for aggravated damages in a *Charter* case? In *Bevis*, the imprisonment was of a very limited duration, and an apology was given very quickly.[121] If aggravated damages were to be awarded in these circumstances, one of the required elements, namely malevolent or egregious conduct, would appear to be absent.

Without such conduct, what would be the cause of any heightened emotional response on the part of the plaintiff? Would the plaintiff's emotional response be heightened just because constitutional rights were violated as well as common law civil rights? Or would the cause of any heightened emotional response be attributed to the fact that *Charter* rights were violated by police officers rather than other civilians. Would the plaintiff suffer greater disappointment, frustration, anger, or loss of dignity because

---

119 See Cooper-Stephenson & Saunders, above note 47 at 56.

120 See note 114, above, for a list of these cases.

121 *Bevis*, above note 35.

a police officer was the cause of the *Charter* violation?[122] Are the wrongful acts of a government official considered to be more egregious than those of a private citizen? Perhaps the psychological impact on the claimant is the result of a combination of all the above-mentioned factors.

Aggravated damages constitute extra compensation to a plaintiff for the mental distress suffered because of the acts and motives of the defendant, but they are not intended to punish. This is so even though both aggravated damages and punitive damages are rooted in the defendant's behaviour. If aggravated damages are theoretically not a neat fit in *Bevis* because of the lack of egregious conduct, if they had been awarded in that case, it would have had to be on the basis of vindication of *Charter* rights. The Nova Scotia Court of Appeal in *Bevis* did emphasize the importance of *Charter* rights and the need to make it clear to the jury that they were important. Because this had not been done, the jury had denied the claim for aggravated damages.

Alternatively, it is clear that in *Bevis* aggravated damages could have served as a substitute for punitive damages, which were not pleaded. Perhaps the Court of Appeal did consider the acts of the police officers to be egregious in nature and even more so because they were police officers rather than because of the nature of the acts themselves.

In non-*Charter* civil actions for personal injury damages, courts have historically been uncertain as to how much direction a jury should have with regard to the calculation of damages amounts. Specific references to similar fact situations and the awards provided therein are very useful as guides, but in many cases they are evidence not of the compensation another jury might have awarded but of what another judge or panel of judges might have thought appropriate for similar injuries. Since personal injury damages in tort cases are now itemized by discreet heads of damages, the comparison of damages awards in different cases can be made item by item. Courts have wavered between a complete ban on references to other damages awards and the compromise of allowing the jury to be informed about the range of awards in other cases.

If we look at the cases in this study, courts, including the Supreme Court of Canada, seem prepared to award compensatory and punitive damages for *Charter* violations, but little has been said about aggravated damages. For this reason alone, *Bevis* is instructive.

---

122 Chief Justice MacDonald questioned whether a jury would "consider it more egregious that these acts were committed by the state through its police officers as opposed to having them committed by ordinary citizens?" (*Bevis* CA, above note 35 at para 63).

iii) Fault Issues in Bevis

The last aspect of the *Bevis*[123] case requiring discussion is the issue of what mental element is required to support *Charter* damages. In the *Bevis* case, a variety of tortious acts were committed, but no real or material harm resulted, either pecuniary or non-pecuniary. From a tort perspective, any damages awarded would have been nominal. Because of the tort-and-*Charter* overlap and the lack of more complete instructions to the jury by the trial judge, it is reasonable to speculate that the jury award of $1,500 to each of the two claimants was, most likely, to compensate for the tortious acts only. Although Moir J seemed to be open to a separate claim for *Charter* damages, the problem of double recovery prevented this.[124] Had a separate award been made, it could still have been based upon the fault evidenced by the tortious acts. That fault, according to Moir J, did not need to involve malice, bad faith, recklessness, or gross negligence as a condition for the award of *Charter* damages under section 24(1). In his view, there was nothing in the plain language of section 24(1) that required such a high standard.[125]

On appeal, MacDonald CJ did not discuss whether the wording of section 24(1) required some element of fault on the part of the defendant to be established by the claimant as a necessary condition for a damages award. However, in response to the claimants' argument that bad faith should be presumed on the part of the police officers, he did declare that "at least in the context of this case, the actions [of the police] must be knowingly or intentionally wrong."[126] This discussion of bad faith was part of a broader discussion of the claimants' request for aggravated damages, rather than a discussion of the fault requirements of section 24(1).

I. *WARD*, TRIAL AND COURT OF APPEAL

The issue in this case,[127] as framed by the Court of Appeal, was whether damages were available as a remedy under section 24(1) of the *Charter* when the *Charter* breach had not been accompanied by a tort and had not been the product of bad faith. The trial judge had decided that damages could be

123 *Bevis*, above note 35.

124 Justice Moir agreed with the authorities, holding "that separate assessment of damages would be duplicitous and would lead to double recovery" (*Bevis* SC, above note 35 at para 5).

125 See *ibid* at para 4.

126 *Bevis* CA, above note 35 at para 82.

127 *Ward*, above note 1.

awarded and cited a number of cases, including *Bevis*[128] and *Bapoo*,[129] where the court had awarded damages without proof of malice, bad faith, or negligence. The majority of the Court of Appeal agreed that bad faith, abusive power, or tortious conduct is not a necessary requirement for an award of *Charter* damages. Justice Low, speaking for the majority of the British Columbia Court of Appeal, noted that there were no appeal decisions (up to the time of the *Ward* appeal) that had dealt with the issue "whether damages are an appropriate remedy under s. 24(1) when, without bad faith and without the commission of any other civil wrong, direct actions by agents of government, while exercising statutory power or duties or implementing government policy, breach a person's *Charter* rights."[130]

Justice Low went on to note the Crown's argument "that there is no remedy in law for an exercise of statutory discretion that is wrongly but honestly exercised" and "that the *Charter* is a statute to which the same rule must apply."[131] To support its argument, the Crown relied upon *Mackin v New Brunswick (Minister of Finance)*[132] and *Wynberg v Ontario*,[133] contending that the *Mackin* decision applied to *Charter* breaches of all kinds with the result that damages were not available in *Ward*.[134] However, Low J disagreed and declared that the *Mackin* decision did not preclude a claim for damages in cases like *Ward*. He also distinguished the *Wynberg* decision, expressing the view that it was clearly restricted to government policy rather than the specific conduct of government agents, which was the focus in *Ward*. As he explained, "[s]triking down government policy on *Charter* grounds is more akin to striking down legislation than it is to the circumstances of the present case."[135]

Justice Saunders, dissenting, expressed the view that awarding damages in situations where no tort had been committed and where there was no evidence of bad faith, abusive power, or negligence was to impose strict liability, even if the purpose of the money award was vindication of *Charter* rights. She argued that section 24(1) *Charter* damages would essentially become a fallback position in case the common law action in tort failed.[136]

---

128 *Bevis*, above note 35.

129 *Bapoo*, above note 38.

130 *Ward* CA, above note 1 at para 49.

131 *Ibid* at paras 54 & 55.

132 *Mackin*, above note 36.

133 (2006), 82 OR (3d) 561 (CA) [*Wynberg*].

134 *Ward* CA, above note 1 at para 58.

135 *Ibid* at para 59.

136 *Ibid* at paras 87–88.

If we look at the actual facts of the *Ward* case, we find that the trial judge, Tysoe J, awarded the plaintiff $5,000 against both the city and the province for strip search violations that had not involved tortious acts, as well as $100 for the seizure of Mr Ward's car and another $5,000 for the unnecessarily long detention. While the latter award also involved the tort of false imprisonment, the wrongful seizure of Mr Ward's car was apparently not considered to be a tortious act. In his pleadings, Mr Ward had alleged wrongful seizure of his car, which, if proven, may very well constitute the tort of conversion. The Court of Appeal noted that the trial judge had not considered this possible tort in his decision and that the Court of Appeal would have to do so only if the province's appeal were successful.[137] As a result, of the three alleged *Charter* violations, only the improper strip search did not involve some element or degree of tortious conduct, although it did involve poor judgment on the part of police officials.

Before its consideration by the Supreme Court of Canada in *Ward*,[138] the issue of a mental element as a prerequisite to a *Charter* damages award had generated different responses, both for and against. As Ducharme J concluded in *Bapoo*, "[t]he case law has not been consistent about whether or not there should be a fault requirement and, if so, what it should be."[139] Those favouring a mental element could argue that if it was not made a prerequisite, then two different standards would be created, one for tort claims and a different one for *Charter* claims, and the *Charter* claim would become a fallback position in case the tort claim failed. This was the position taken by Saunders JA in *Ward*.[140] And to eliminate fault of some sort as a prerequisite to *Charter* damages would be to impose strict liability, as Saunders JA also argued in her dissent in *Ward*.[141]

The arguments against the need for some form of fault or state of mind of the defendant are several and varied. One argument stresses the fact that the *Charter* as a whole focuses on the consequences of state action, that is, was there a violation of the *Charter*, rather than on the underlying intent of the defendant or purpose of the defendant's actions.[142] One response to this argument might be that this approach is more relevant to the issue whether there was a violation of *Charter* rights initially rather than the question whether damages are an appropriate and just remedy. A second

---

137 *Ibid* at para 33.
138 *Ward* SCC, above note 1.
139 *Bapoo*, above note 38 at para 186.
140 *Ward* CA, above note 1 at para 87.
141 *Ibid* at para 88.
142 This was the observation of Ducharme J in *Bapoo*, above note 38 at para 194.

argument suggests that to require the plaintiff to prove some kind of mental state of the defendant would create the risk of eliminating effective remedies for *Charter* breaches.[143] A third argument against the need for a mental element is that malice, bad faith, gross negligence, or wilful disregard of *Charter* rights should be reserved for the question or issue of punitive damages, rather than considered as a necessary prerequisite for compensatory damages. One counter-argument in favour of a fault requirement points out that *Charter* damages are not the primary remedy[144] and should not be automatically granted upon breach.[145] Allowing *Charter* damages without some filter, this argument suggests, would have a chilling effect upon government conduct.

It was against this background that McLachlin CJ approached the issue of *Charter* damages in *Ward*.

J. CONCLUDING OBSERVATIONS

In terms of the number of *Charter* damages cases per year, the frequency rate during the first survey period was 1.9 per year (twenty-one cases in eleven years). During the second period, the frequency rate increased to 3.3 per year (fifty cases in fifteen years), not a dramatic increase but worth noting. The success rate in the second period decreased slightly by 4 percentage points (38 to 34 percent) with a consequent increase in the rejection rate. A different trend is noted in the average award amount (excluding anomalies), which increased by $7,697.

Sections 7, 8, or 9 of the *Charter* consistently represented the basis for an action for damages pursuant to section 24(1) in both periods, but the second period did show an increase in damages awards based on a violation of section 15. There continued to be a lack of any correlation between the *Charter* section violated and the probability of a successful claim for *Charter* damages.

The question or issue of fault emerged as the most frequently debated issue in the second survey period, being an issue in approximately 84 percent

143 Such a view was expressed by Ducharme J in *Bapoo*, *ibid*, voicing his concern that requiring the plaintiff to prove some kind of state of mind independent of the *Charter* breach, particularly malice, would make it very difficult for a plaintiff to succeed in a *Charter* damages claim.

144 As was pointed out by the Supreme Court in *RJR – MacDonald*, above note 40.

145 This view was expressed by the court in *Lagiorgia v Canada*, [1985] 1 FC 438 (TD), rev'd in part [1987] 3 FC 28 (CA), leave to appeal to SCC refused (1988), 61 CR (3d) xxviii.

of the cases. This represented a considerable increase over the first period. However, the high standard of fault, expressed by the courts as malice or *mala fides*, was applied in slightly fewer cases in the period 1995–2010 (30 percent) than in the first eleven years (1984–94), which had seen the high standard applied in 33 percent of the cases.

The tort-and-*Charter* conflict and the problem of double compensation continued to be an issue but in far fewer cases than in the first period. The appropriateness of allowing the common law defence of qualified immunity engaged the attention of Canada's highest court in two cases in the early years of the second period.[146] The decisions in these cases no doubt helped reduce the uncertainty surrounding the applicability of the defence to *Charter* damages claims and perhaps reduced the number of cases in which it was raised in the later years of the period. Finally, the second period saw the issue of *Charter* damages being presented to a jury for the first time in *Bevis*[147] — a new problem for trial judges.

---

146 *Guimond*, above note 36; *Mackin*, above note 36.

147 *Bevis*, above note 35.

Chapter 4

Supreme Court of Canada Decisions

1995–2010

A. INTRODUCTION

In the fifteen years that followed its 1994 decision in *RJR – MacDonald Inc v Canada (AG)*,[1] Canada's highest court continued to discuss the relationship between section 52(1) of the *Constitution Act, 1982*[2] and section 24(1) of the *Canadian Charter of Rights and Freedoms*,[3] and the issue of concurrent remedies. In what appears to be the final word on the issue, the Supreme Court of Canada in *R v Ferguson*[4] again tried to clarify the relationship between the two sections by pointing out that they serve different remedial purposes. The Court explained as follows:

> Section 24(1) has generally been seen — at least until now — as providing a case-by-case remedy for unconstitutional acts of government agents operating under lawful schemes whose constitutionality is not challenged. The other remedy section, s. 52(1) of the *Constitution Act, 1982*, confers no discretion on judges. It simply provides that laws that are inconsistent with the *Charter* are of no force and effect to the extent of that inconsistency . . . .[5]

In other words, section 24(1) provides remedies for unconstitutional actions of government officials while section 52(1) provides a remedy for unconstitutional laws. As to the related problem of concurrent remedies under

1 [1994] 1 SCR 311.

2 Being Schedule B to the *Canada Act 1982* (UK), 1982, c 11.

3 Part I of the *Constitution Act, 1982*, being Schedule B to the *Canada Act 1982* (UK), 1982, c 11 [*Charter*].

4 2008 SCC 6 [*Ferguson*].

5 *Ibid* at para 35, McLachlin CJ.

these two sections, the Supreme Court in *R v Demers* had in 2004, four years before the *Ferguson* decision, declared, "In our view, there is no reason to revisit the wisdom of the *Schachter* rule in the present case."[6]

The issue of appropriate jurisdiction to award *Charter* damages continued to arise not only in relation to provincial offences courts in Ontario[7] but also in relation to administrative tribunals.[8] In both situations, the Supreme Court held that the institution had jurisdiction to award *Charter* damages.

B. PRINCIPLES OF INTERPRETATION

During the period under review, the Supreme Court of Canada decided two cases that not only provided useful directions as to the proper approach to the interpretation of section 24(1) but also described the characteristics of "an appropriate and just" remedy. In both *Ontario v 974649 Ontario Inc*[9] and *Doucet-Boudreau v Nova Scotia (Minister of Education)*,[10] the Supreme Court emphasized the importance of taking a purposive approach to both the *Charter* as a whole and section 24(1) in particular. However, in the latter case, the Court went further by suggesting what might be the hallmarks of an appropriate and just remedy.[11]

Justices Iacobucci and Arbour, speaking for the majority, began by emphasizing the general objectives and aims of the *Charter* remedies generally. They then suggested that a remedy that would be considered appropriate and just would involve the following characteristics: (1) it would meaningfully vindicate the rights and freedoms of the claimants, (2) it would employ means that are legitimate within the framework of our constitutional democracy, (3) it would be a judicial remedy that vindicates the right while involving the function and powers of the court, and (4) it would be fair to

---

6 2004 SCC 46 at para 62 [*Demers*], Iacobucci and Bastarache JJ. Speaking for the Court, the two justices explained that while the rule in *Schachter v Canada*, [1992] 2 SCR 679, precluded courts from combining retroactive remedies (including damages) under s 24(1) with s 52 remedies, it did not prevent a court from awarding prospective remedies under s 24(1) in conjunction with s 52 remedies. It should be noted that the remedy requested in *Demers* was a stay of proceedings rather than *Charter* damages.

7 See *Ontario v 974649 Ontario Inc*, 2001 SCC 81 [*974649 Ontario*].

8 See *Weber v Ontario Hydro*, [1995] 2 SCR 929.

9 *974649 Ontario*, above note 7.

10 2003 SCC 62.

11 *Ibid* at paras 54–58.

the party against whom the order is made.[12] It is interesting to note that vindication is an element in two of the four characteristics but that there is no mention of deterrence.

C. QUALIFIED IMMUNITY DEFENCE

In addition to issues involving concurrent remedies and the proper interpretive approach to section 24(1), the Supreme Court of Canada faced an additional issue during the second survey period. This was the very relevant question whether the Crown could raise the defence of immunity to liability claims founded upon *Charter* violations. The general rule of Canadian public law, as created by the common law, provides that "absent conduct that is clearly wrong, in bad faith or an abuse of power, the courts will not award damages for the harm suffered as a result of the mere enactment or application of a law that is subsequently declared to be unconstitutional . . . ."[13] This limited or qualified immunity provided by the common law was recognized and applied in several pre-*Charter* Supreme Court decisions as well as early trial decisions involving claims for damages under section 24(1).[14] In these early *Charter* cases, in the period from 1984 to 1995, the scope and range of the immunity granted varied as did the content, in terms of fault or other mental elements that might be required. Overall, the immunity provided by Canadian general public law was limited both in scope and in content.

1) The American Doctrine of Qualified Immunity

American constitutional jurisprudence has developed a so-called qualified immunity defence, which calls for a limited immunity from liability for government officials who, acting in good faith and exercising reasonable discretion, nevertheless violate a person's constitutional rights. As the US

12 *Ibid.*

13 This is the rule as formulated by the Supreme Court in *Mackin v New Brunswick (Minister of Finance)*, 2002 SCC 13 at para 78 [*Mackin*]. It reflects the Court's earlier decisions in *Welbridge Holdings Ltd v Greater Winnipeg*, [1971] SCR 957 [*Welbridge*], and *Central Canada Potash Co Ltd v Government of Saskatchewan*, [1979] 1 SCR 42 [*Canada Potash*].

14 In addition to *Welbridge*, *ibid*, and *Canada Potash*, *ibid*, there are several trial decisions in which the immunity defence appears to have been raised and applied by the court. In these cases, enforcement officials had relied upon erroneous or faulty judicial authorization such as arrest warrants: see *Scorpio Rising Software Inc v Saskatchewan* (AG) (1986), 46 Sask R 230 (QB); *R v BB* (1986), 69 AR 203 (Prov Ct).

Supreme Court explained in *Harlow v Fitzgerald*, "officials performing discretionary functions, generally are shielded from liability for civil damages insofar as their conduct does not violate clearly established statutory or constitutional rights of which a reasonable person would have known."[15]

The key features of the American doctrine are as follows: (1) it applies to situations where government officials are exercising administrative discretion, (2) that discretion must be exercised reasonably and in good faith, and (3) the official must not be aware that his actions are violating a person's constitutional rights. If the official knew or should have known that a violation would occur, the courts will deny immunity.[16]

2) Qualified Immunity: Four Basic Questions

Any court considering whether to recognize and apply a defence of qualified immunity has to consider four interrelated questions.[17] First, is there now in Canadian jurisprudence any doctrine that may be described as a qualified immunity? And if not, should one be developed? Second, to what categories of government officials should the immunity apply? Third, to what government functions should the immunity apply? And, fourth, what are the conditions that must be met to allow the defence to be applied, including the required state of mind of the government official involved, and, conversely, what conditions would prevent the immunity from being available? The first question addresses the existence of the immunity defence while the second and third questions address the scope or range of that defence in terms of any potential defendants and their functions. The last question addresses the content of the doctrine in the sense of what fault or mental element will be required.

---

15 457 US 800 at 818 (1982).

16 Professor Pilkington discusses some of these features in her article "Damages as a Remedy for Infringement of the *Canadian Charter of Rights and Freedoms*" (1984) 62:4 *Canadian Bar Review* 517 at 557–58.

17 These questions, as well as others, are posed by Professor Cooper-Stephenson in his book *Charter Damages Claims* (Toronto: Carswell, 1990) at 316. Cooper-Stephenson also points out that "[b]y contrast with absolute immunity, the qualified immunity doctrine involves a larger number of complex and integrated issues" (*ibid* at 315).

3) Pre-*Charter* Constitutional Jurisprudence in Canada and the American Doctrine of Qualified Immunity

In 1989, the Ontario High Court of Justice was considering the case of *Jane Doe v Commissioners of Police*.[18] The Crown in this case attempted to raise the defence or principle of qualified immunity from suit available to public officials under US decisions known as the "good faith" or "qualified immunity" defence. Justice Henry rejected the Crown argument, declaring that "there is no such principle of immunity provided as an exception to the *Charter*."[19]

The immunity claimed in this case was from liability arising from the failure of police officers, a chief of police, and a board of police commissioners to warn the plaintiff of a serial rapist and the fact that they were using her as bait. In rejecting the immunity defence, Henry J observed that the American defence was "in essence the principle that government officials are not liable to action for their decisions carried out in the bona fide exercise of their discretion."[20] He further noted that in Canada this was a matter for justification under section 1 of the *Charter* and not activity protected by any qualified immunity defence.[21]

4) The Claim of Right Defence

Although, as Henry J declared in *Doe*, Canadian jurisprudence did not recognize the doctrine of qualified immunity, at least not as proclaimed by US jurisprudence, there did exist at the time of the *Doe* decision a common law defence that was recognized by Canadian courts in constitutional cases and known as "claim of right" or "colour of right."[22] The Crown could invoke this defence in situations where the government, or an official, had purported to act pursuant to a statute or rule that was later found to be unconstitutional. The defence was also available when a government had acted in an executive or administrative capacity (or had failed to act) on the mistaken view that its conduct did not violate provisions of the *Charter*. The clearest expression of the defence of claim of right was provided by Martland J in *Central Canada Potash Co Ltd v Government of Saskatchewan*: "In my opinion it would be unfortunate, in a federal state such as Canada, if

18 (1989), 58 DLR (4th) 396 (Ont HCJ) [*Doe*].

19 *Ibid* at 435.

20 *Ibid*.

21 *Ibid*.

22 *Ibid*. This defence is discussed at some length by Cooper-Stephenson, above note 17 at 322–23.

it were to be held that a government official, charged with the enforcement of legislation, could be held to be guilty of intimidation because of his enforcement of the statute whenever a statute whose provisions he is under a duty to enforce is subsequently held to be *ultra vires*."[23]

In Canadian law, government and its officials are also protected from liability and negligence when acting in a legislative capacity or exercising statutory discretion.[24] This protection is justified on the basis that in making policy choices, public officials owe a duty of care to the public but not to individual citizens. This immunity covers discretionary public policy choices but not operational or implementational choices or discretion. This raises the question whether such a dichotomy, which governs ordinary civil suits, should also be available in cases involving *Charter* violations.

5) The *De Facto* Doctrine

Another doctrine, known as the *de facto* (validity) doctrine, is also involved in situations where legislation is declared to be unconstitutional. Said to be of ancient and venerable origin, with the first English case recorded in 1431, the doctrine was recognized by the Romans and has long been accepted in Canada.[25] It is a doctrine with several different facets to it. Primarily a doctrine to maintain the supremacy of the rule of law by preventing a vacuum in the legal system from occurring, it also acts to protect the rights, obligations, and interests of those who are affected by the invalid legislation from the effects of the acts of those officials implementing the legislation. The third aspect of the *de facto* doctrine protects government officials from liability by imparting validity to their official acts. These officials, however, must hold office or exercise lawfully existing offices, of whatever nature, in situations where the performance of their official acts or functions is for the benefit of the public. The doctrine was raised in arguments by intervenors

---

23 *Canada Potash*, above note 13 at 90.

24 See *Welbridge*, above note 13.

25 The Supreme Court provides the doctrine's historical background in *Re Manitoba Language Rights*, [1985] 1 SCR 721 at 755, where the Court also makes reference to its earlier decision in *O'Neil v AG of Canada* (1896), 26 SCR 122. The seminal explanation and definition of the *de facto* doctrine is provided by Judge Albert Constantineau in his book *A Treatise on the* De Facto *Doctrine: In Its Relation to Public Officers and Public Corporations Based upon the English, American, and Canadian Cases Including Comments upon Extraordinary Legal Remedies in Reference to the Trial of Title to Office, and Corporate Existence* (Toronto: Canada Law Book, 1910), which the Supreme Court references in *Re Manitoba Language Rights*, *ibid*.

in *Re Manitoba Language Rights*[26] and accepted and applied by the Supreme Court of Canada to partially resolve the dilemma caused by an earlier declaration of the Court in *AG of Manitoba v Forest*[27] that the Manitoba government had failed to comply with its constitutional duty under section 23 of the *Manitoba Act, 1870*[28] to enact bilingual legislation. As a result of the *Forest* decision, all unilingual statutes enacted since 1890 in Manitoba were to be considered unconstitutional. The Court in *Re Manitoba Language Rights* used the *de facto* doctrine, together with the doctrine of *res judicata* and the doctrine of necessity, to develop a solution whereby the offending statutes were deemed to be valid until such times as the Manitoba legislature could enact the proper legislation. The doctrine was also referred to and applied by the Ontario Divisional Court in the more recent case of *Crown Trust Co v Ontario*[29] as one of several defences to a claim for *Charter* damages.

6) *Guimond v Quebec (AG)*

It was against this background that Gonthier J on behalf of the Supreme Court of Canada approached the issue of crown liability in *Guimond v Quebec (AG)*.[30] The main issue in this case was whether the trial judge had exercised his discretion properly by not authorizing the commencement of a class action in Quebec. It was the plaintiff's contention that the sentencing provisions of the Quebec *Code of Penal Procedure*[31] and its predecessor, the *Summary Convictions Act*,[32] infringed the Canadian *Charter*[33] and the Quebec *Charter of Human Rights and Freedoms*.[34] A decision on the main issue of authorization for a class action depended upon the plaintiff's establishing a viable action for damages against the Crown. If there was no legal basis for a damages claim then the class action would fail. The trial judge had exercised his discretion and rejected the application for a class action authorization. The Court of Appeal, by majority decision, reversed the trial judge, holding that the circumstances did raise an appearance of a right

26 *Re Manitoba Language Rights, ibid.*
27 [1979] 2 SCR 1032 [*Forest*].
28 33 Vict, c 3.
29 (1986), 54 OR (2d) 79 (Div Ct) [*Crown Trust*].
30 [1996] 3 SCR 347 [*Guimond*].
31 RSQ, c C-25.1.
32 RSQ, c P-15.
33 *Charter*, above note 3.
34 RSQ 1975, c C-12.

to claim damages for breach of *Charter* guarantees.[35] However, Delisle J dissented. In his dissent, he referred to Martland J's statement in *Canada Potash*[36] rejecting liability and noted, in addition, that awarding damages would run counter to the *de facto* doctrine. He was also unable to interpret the *Schachter v Canada*[37] decision as permitting a remedy in damages in the situation of a statute held to be unconstitutional after the fact, which was the case in *Guimond*.[38]

Justice Gonthier observed that the crux of the respondent's application was a claim for damages based upon an allegation of constitutional invalidity. The defence of qualified immunity had been raised by the Crown in response to the damages claim. When considering the applicability of this defence to *Charter* cases, Gonthier J first reviewed a number of authorities concerned with the liability of the Crown for damages resulting from the enactment of laws later found to be unconstitutional. His review included the pre-*Charter* decisions of the Supreme Court in *Welbridge*[39] and *Canada Potash*[40] and the comments of Canadian legal academics[41] as well as two post-*Charter* cases.[42]

Justice Gonthier noted that the Supreme Court had, in both *Welbridge* and *Canada Potash*, clearly enunciated the general principle of public law that an action in tort for civil damages would not lie against the Crown.[43] It should be noted at this point that the common law immunity principle in *Welbridge* was applied to a law-making body exercising a legislative function whereas in *Canada Potash* the immunity was applied to a government official (a deputy minister) who had been attempting to enforce or implement statutory powers later declared to be unconstitutional. As a result of his review, Gonthier J concluded the following:

---

35 (1995), 123 DLR (4th) 236 [*Guimond* CA].

36 *Canada Potash*, above note 13 at 90.

37 [1992] 2 SCR 679 [*Schachter*].

38 Justice Delisle's dissenting judgment is found at *Guimond* CA, above note 35 at 252–54.

39 *Welbridge*, above note 13.

40 *Canada Potash*, above note 13.

41 Patrice Garant, *Droit administrative*, 3e ed (Cowansville, Quebec: Éditions Yvon Blais, 1991) vol 2; Cooper-Stephenson, above note 17; Marilyn L Pilkington, "Monetary Redress for *Charter* Infringement" in Robert J Sharpe, ed, *Charter Litigation* (Toronto: Butterworths, 1987) 307 at 319–20.

42 *Re Manitoba Language Rights*, above note 25; *Crown Trust*, above note 29.

43 *Guimond*, above note 30 at para 13.

1) Academic commentators were generally of the view that the claim of right defence applied with equal force under section 24(1).[44]
2) *Charter* jurisprudence supported the view that there was no right to compensation when the *Charter* violation resulted from a statute later declared to be unconstitutional.[45]
3) Several courts had relied upon the *de facto* doctrine to deny an action for *Charter* damages arising from an unconstitutional statute.[46]
4) No claim for damages in the present case was possible because the claimant had based his claim upon a bare allegation of unconstitutionality. The Supreme Court had ruled in the *Schachter* case, two years earlier, that damages would only rarely be granted with a declaration of invalidity. Since no allegation of bad faith or malice had been made, the general rule of *Schachter* applied to deny damages.[47]

The *Guimond* decision demonstrates an interesting interplay between the rule in *Schachter*,[48] which deals primarily with concurrent remedies under section 52(1) and section 24(1), and the problem of retroactivity and the defence of qualified immunity. One rare exception to the general *Schachter* rule involves the situation where a Crown actor relying upon a presumed valid statute acts in some malicious manner. In this situation, the *Schachter* rule or principle and the defence of qualified immunity become intertwined.

Justice Gonthier's decision in *Guimond* raises several important issues, all of which relate to the defence of qualified immunity. By making reference to the claim of right defence as well as the *de facto* principle and the qualified immunity defence, Gonthier J makes it difficult to determine, at this stage, whether the Supreme Court in *Guimond* considered the three defences to be separate and distinct from each other or to be just variations of the principle embodied in the term "qualified immunity." Another question that arises is whether all three terms are merely different verbal descriptions of the pre-*Charter* common law principle of public law immunity, as expressed by the Supreme Court in the *Welbridge*[49] and *Canada Potash*[50] cases. A further question that arises from the *Guimond* decision is whether

44 *Ibid* at para 15.

45 *Ibid* at para 16.

46 *Ibid* at paras 16 & 17. These cases were *Re Manitoba Language Rights*, above note 25, and *Crown Trust*, above note 29.

47 *Guimond*, above note 30 at para 19.

48 *Schachter*, above note 37.

49 *Welbridge*, above note 13.

50 *Canada Potash*, above note 13.

the term "qualified immunity" when used in the context of Canadian *Charter* cases is identical to the American concept of "qualified immunity" in its scope of application. As previously noted, the American concept is broader in scope in that it is not restricted to situations involving a presumed constitutionally valid statute that is later declared to be invalid. These issues received some clarification six years later when the Supreme Court once more grappled with the concept of qualified immunity.

7) *Mackin v New Brunswick (Minister of Finance)*

The issue of Crown immunity as a defence came before the Supreme Court of Canada a second time in the case of *Mackin v New Brunswick (Minister of Finance)* in 2002.[51] The main issue in this case was whether the New Brunswick legislature's abolition of the position of supernumerary judge of the Provincial Court of New Brunswick contravened the constitutional guarantees of judicial independence protected by section 11(d) of the *Charter* and the preamble to the *Constitution Act, 1867*. There were two incidental issues in this case as well. One was whether the respondent should be awarded damages for the *Charter* violation, and the other was whether costs should be ordered on a solicitor-client basis or not. The trial judge relied upon the decisions in *Schachter*[52] and *Guimond*[53] and found no evidence of bad faith or corrupt motives.[54] He therefore denied the *Charter* claim. The Court of Appeal agreed with the trial judge that the actions of the provincial government were a violation of the concept of judicial independence.[55] However, by a majority, the court declared that the general rule of public law as set out in *Guimond*, which held that damages will not be awarded for the enactment of legislation later declared to be unconstitutional except in the event of bad faith or other wrongful conduct of government institutions, should not apply. There was no mention by members of the Court of Appeal of the claim of right defence, qualified immunity, or the *de facto* doctrine.

The case was appealed to the Supreme Court, and again Gonthier J delivered the judgment of the Court, as he had in *Guimond*. He began his analysis of the damages issue by referring to the earlier cases of *Welbridge*,[56] *Canada*

---

51 *Mackin*, above note 13.
52 *Schachter*, above note 37.
53 *Guimond*, above note 30.
54 (1998), 202 NBR (2d) 324 (QB), Deschênes J.
55 (1999), 40 CPC (4th) 107 (NBCA) [*Mackin* CA].
56 *Welbridge*, above note 13.

Potash,[57] and *Crown Trust*,[58] as well as the Court's decision in *Guimond*. Using these as a backdrop, after once again quoting the declaration of Lamer J in *Schachter*,[59] Gonthier J concluded that application of the principles represented by these cases made clear that "the respondents are not entitled to damages merely because the enactment of Bill 7 was unconstitutional."[60] Something more than proof that unconstitutional legislation had been enacted was required.[61]

In his decision, Gonthier J then expressed a number of relevant observations and comments about the defence of qualified immunity and its role and function in Canadian jurisprudence. When taken together, they provide a very helpful summary of the legal situation vis-à-vis Crown immunity at the time of the *Mackin* case.[62] They may be summarized as follows:

1) Both public officials and legislative bodies enjoy limited immunity from civil liability based on the fact that a legislative instrument is involved.
2) The *Mackin* case was similar to *Welbridge* in that the offending actor was a government institution rather than an official of government.
3) Limited immunity gives the government a means of creating a balance between the protection of constitutional rights and the need for effective government.
4) In situations like *Mackin*, the general rule of public law, based upon Supreme Court decisions such as *Welbridge* and *Canada Potash*, applies and holds that absent conduct that is clearly wrong, in bad faith, or an abuse of power courts will not award damages for harm suffered as a result of the mere enactment or application of a law that is later declared unconstitutional.
5) The reason underlying the general principle of public law, that is, the qualifying conditions that enable the Crown to claim immunity from liability, is equally relevant and applicable to the *Charter*. These conditions or qualifications require that the Crown, whether represented by institutions or officials, must act in good faith and "respect the 'established and indisputable' laws that define the constitutional rights of

57 *Canada Potash*, above note 13.
58 *Crown Trust*, above note 29.
59 *Schachter*, above note 37 at 720.
60 *Mackin*, above note 13 at para 82.
61 *Ibid*. This comment by Gonthier J was probably in response to the position taken by the majority in the Court of Appeal decision.
62 The relevant comments may be found at *Mackin*, above note 13 at paras 78–82.

individuals."[63] That immunity will be lost if government actors engage in conduct that is clearly wrong, in bad faith, or an abuse of power.

6) As was held in *Guimond*, a plaintiff is no longer restricted to an action based upon the general law of civil liability (private law) but, in theory, can bring an action for both compensatory and punitive damages by way of appropriate remedy under the *Charter*.

Several observations seem in order. First, both in the individual judgments of the members of the Court of Appeal in *Mackin*[64] and in the judgment of Gonthier J for the Supreme Court, there is no mention of the claim of right defence or the *de facto* doctrine. The nature or source of the limited immunity defence referred to by the Supreme Court in *Mackin*, as applicable in *Charter* cases, appears to be the general rule of public law developed by the common law as expressed in *Welbridge* and *Canada Potash*. When Gonthier J does lapse into a reference to qualified immunity, he is apparently using the term interchangeably with limited immunity. There is no doubt now, if there ever was after the *Guimond*[65] decision, that the American doctrine of qualified immunity is not being adopted by the Supreme Court. Similarly, it would seem that specific doctrines such as claim of right and *de facto* are subsumed under the umbrella term used by the Court in *Mackin*, namely, limited immunity.

If we return to the four basic questions that were raised about the defence of qualified immunity earlier in this chapter,[66] we can now say that as a result of the Supreme Court's decisions in *Guimond* and *Mackin*, the defence, whether we call it limited immunity or qualified immunity, is applicable in Canada. Second, we can affirm that the defence can be raised by ministers of the Crown[67] or officials of administrative bodies such as school boards.[68] Insofar as government functions are concerned, immunity applies to legislative functions[69] as well as executive, administrative,[70] and quasi-judicial functions.[71]

---

63 *Ibid* at para 79.

64 *Mackin* CA, above note 55.

65 *Guimond*, above note 30.

66 See Section C(2), above in this chapter.

67 See *Canada Potash*, above note 13; *Seniuk v Saskatchewan (Minister of Justice)* (1995), 133 Sask R 115 (QB) [*Seniuk*].

68 See *Lewis v School District No 41 (Burnaby)* (1992), 71 BCLR (2d) 183 (SC); *McCorkell v Riverview Hospital Review Bd* (1993), 104 DLR (4th) 391 at 394–95 [*McCorkell*].

69 See *Re Manitoba Language Rights*, above note 25.

70 See *Canada Potash*, above note 13; *Seniuk*, above note 67.

71 See *McCorkell*, above note 68; *Crown Trust*, above note 29.

The answer to the fourth question, that is, what conditions must be established, including the state of mind of government officials, before the defence can apply, is more complicated because of the diverse language used by the courts to describe these conditions. In *Mackin*, Gonthier J, after his review of the authorities, noted the different language used to describe the standard of fault that, if proven by the plaintiff, would overcome or neutralize the defence of qualified immunity. Examples mentioned by Gonthier J included the following: "conduct that is clearly wrong, in bad faith or an abuse of power"; acting "negligently, in bad faith or by abusing its powers"; and displaying "negligence, bad faith or wilful blindness with respect to its constitutional obligations at that time."[72] Conversely, if the defendant can establish that its power or authority was exercised "in good faith" or that it acted "in good faith and without abusing" its power, the qualified immunity defence could be invoked successfully.[73]

In the *Mackin* case, the Court applied the standard of general public law, namely, "conduct that is clearly wrong, in bad faith, or an abuse of power," as the threshold that would render the qualified or limited immunity defence inoperative. Wrongful conduct is a somewhat imprecise term because it can encompass legally wrong, or tortious, acts as well as morally wrong but not necessarily legally prohibited acts. It can, for example, include the negligence alleged in *Welbridge*[74] and the tortious conduct of the deputy minister in *Canada Potash*[75] as well as actions that involve some mental element considered to be wrong such as an ulterior motive or an intention to perform a wrongful or tortious act. The mental element alone and unaccompanied by action may be wrong morally but not actionable legally. Bad faith implies acts undertaken to mislead another party or to neglect the fulfillment of some obligation, not through an honest mistake. Good faith, on the other hand, implies the absence of intent to take advantage of or defraud another party, with no ulterior motive. To act in good faith is to act openly, fairly, and honestly.[76] As far as abuse of power is concerned, there is a recognized tort of misfeasance in office. Any damage caused by malicious or negligent exercise of statutory powers by a statutory corporation or public officer is

72 *Mackin*, above note 13 at paras 79 and 82.

73 *Ibid* at para 79.

74 *Welbridge*, above note 13.

75 *Canada Potash*, above note 13.

76 John A Yogis, *Canadian Law Dictionary* (Woodbury, NY: Barron's Educational Series, 1983) *sub verbo* "good faith" at 96. Yogis also states that the existence of negligence is irrelevant.

actionable as misfeasance.[77] However, it must be proven that the defendant knew she was acting in an *ultra vires* manner.[78]

The limited immunity defence as developed by the general public law jurisprudence, as previously explained, has elements involving actions that viewed objectively can be considered wrong or at fault and also elements involving subjective states of mind such as ulterior motive or the intention to perform a wrongful act.[79] The inclination of courts, as reflected in their decisions on *Charter* damages, suggests that as far as wrongful acts are concerned, they require more than mere negligence, carelessness, or reasonable error to satisfy the objective part or element of the new standard of limited immunity. As stated in *Mackin*, this defence is restricted in its application to cases involving constitutionally valid statutes or laws later declared to be invalid.[80]

8) Pressure to Extend Crown Immunity

As a postscript to the *Guimond*[81] and *Mackin*[82] decisions, it is worth noting the pressure on courts to extend the defence of qualified or limited immunity to non-statutory situations. For example, the Federal Court of Appeal in *Pearson v Canada*[83] extended the application of the defence to officials acting on the basis of what they thought were valid common law principles while the Ontario Court of Appeal in *Wynberg v Ontario*[84] applied the defence to a situation involving improper implementation of a valid statute by government officials. By so doing, the Ontario court appeared to be adopting the American version of qualified immunity, an approach not adopted by the Supreme Court of Canada.[85] The argument for extending the qualified immunity defence to non-statutory situations is clearly articulated by the Manitoba Court of Queen's Bench in *Neufeld v Manitoba*.[86] The court in this case explained, "Governments should be free to carry out their mandate without concern that taxpayers will ultimately face a huge liability. There-

77 Sir John Salmond, Robert Francis Vere Heuston, & RA Buckley, *Salmond and Heuston on the Law of Torts*, 19th ed (London: Sweet & Maxwell, 1987) at 43.
78 *Ibid.*
79 *Mackin*, above note 13 at para 79.
80 *Ibid.*
81 *Guimond*, above note 30.
82 *Mackin*, above note 13.
83 2007 FCA 380, leave to appeal to SCC refused, [2008] SCCA No 299.
84 (2006), 82 OR (3d) 561 (CA).
85 See *Guimond*, above note 30; *Mackin*, above note 13.
86 2001 MBQB 201, aff'd but not on the damages issue 2002 MBCA 123.

fore, the fact that the government action called into question was not pursuant to legislation does not mean that the policy justification is not applicable here."[87] The Manitoba Court of Appeal did not agree and reversed the trial judge on the issue of damages.[88]

As to the issue of content and the proper fault requirement, the Ontario trial court in *Hawley v Bapoo*[89] suggested that the proper standard to prevent the application of the immunity defence was something less than malice or bad faith. Justice Ducharme found support for his suggestion in the variety of language Gonthier J had used in *Mackin* to explain what the proper standard of fault should be, a standard that included negligence. As a result, Ducharme J felt justified in concluding as follows: "Therefore, even in a case involving legislative authorization, it seems that negligent action might be open to a claim for damages."[90] Clearly, there were still immunity issues to be resolved.

---

87 *Ibid* at para 67.

88 2002 MBCA 123.

89 (2005), 76 OR (3d) 649 (SCJ), var'd 2007 ONCA 503.

90 *Ibid* at para 190.

Chapter 5

Common Law Damages

The Basis for Charter *Damages or Only a Guide?*

A. INTRODUCTION

Once courts made the decision that money compensation was an "appropriate and just remedy" for violations of the *Canadian Charter of Rights and Freedoms*,[1] they then had to face questions about the nature of such damages. What form would they take, what purposes would they serve, and how would they be computed? The principles underlying common law damages were familiar and known to the judiciary, but would common law damages be a suitable template from which to develop *Charter* damages? How binding or persuasive should common law damages principles be? Certainly, the judiciary recognized that civil wrongs were of a different order or status than breaches of fundamental *Charter* rights,[2] but how would this distinction

1 Part I of the *Constitution Act, 1982*, being Schedule B to the *Canada Act 1982* (UK), 1982, c 11 [*Charter*].

2 Justice Wilson, dissenting, in *McKinney v University of Guelph*, [1990] 3 SCR 229 at 408, raised the issue most directly when she declared, ". . . I believe that different considerations respecting appropriate remedial relief should prevail when constitutional rights and freedoms as opposed to common law rights are at stake." In *R v Hamill* (1984), 13 DLR (4th) 275 at 297 (BCCA), Esson JA suggested, "It is arguable that, in granting civil remedies for Charter breaches, courts should assess damages at more substantial levels than have prevailed for trespasses arising out of illegal entry." Justice Ducharme, the trial judge in *Hawley v Bapoo* (2005), 76 OR (3d) 649 at 734, var'd 2007 ONCA 503 [*Bapoo*], expressed the view that *Charter* damages were not necessarily tied, in terms of the amount of compensation awarded, to civil award amounts. Finally, the Nova Scotia Court of Appeal in *Bevis v CTV Inc (cob ATV/CTV)*, 2006 NSCA 56, var'g 2004 NSSC 247, stressed the need for trial judges to

affect judicial approaches to more specific damages issues such as consequential losses or *per se* violations of the *Charter*?

B. *PER SE* DAMAGES

The issue of *per se* damages was the subject of academic discussion and comment shortly after the enactment of the *Charter.* In a seminal article published in 1984, Professor Pilkington posed the question whether courts would be prepared to compensate victims of *Charter* violations in situations where the plaintiff suffered no consequential harm, loss, or injury as a result of the *Charter* violation.[3] In other words, would the courts entertain the idea of a *Charter* violation that was actionable *per se*? If they did, how would they determine the question of damages in these situations? For ease of reference, damages awarded in these situations will be referred to as damages *per se* or *per se* damages.

At common law, the general rule is that no legal wrong is established unless damages are proven to be a consequence of the defendant's actions. But there are some exceptions to the general rule, usually involving old tort actions designed to protect interests in personal security (such as assault and battery) or in ownership or possession of property, both real and personal. In these old actions, breach of an obligation is all that is necessary to support a damages award. If proven, the court may award nominal compensation for the wrong done to the plaintiff.[4] Proof of harm or injury is un-

---

make clear in their instructions to the jury the importance of *Charter* rights. In several other cases, courts or counsel have made reference to "constitutional torts" but without clearly drawing attention to any relevant differences between civil torts and "constitutional torts": see, for example, *McGillivary v New Brunswick* (1993), 140 NBR (2d) 365 at paras 27 & 28 (QB), aff'd (1994), 116 DLR (4th) 104 (CA); *Ferri v Ontario (AG)*, [2006] OJ No 710 at para 108 (SCJ), var'd 2007 ONCA 79; *Bapoo, ibid* at para 185.

3 Marilyn L Pilkington, "Damages as a Remedy for Infringement of the Canadian Charter of Rights and Freedoms" (1984) 62:4 *Canadian Bar Review* 517 at 567.

4 Nominal damages have been defined as the "amount (usually a trivial sum) paid to the plaintiff who has proved the infraction of a legal right but has failed to prove what damage, if any, was caused thereby . . . *Hudson's Bay Oil & Gas Co. Ltd. v. Dynamic Petroleums Ltd.* (1957), 26 W.W.R. 504 (Alta S.C.)" (John A Yogis, *Canadian Law Dictionary* (Woodbury, NY: Barron's Educational Series, 1983) at 59) and, to similar effect, as a "trifling sum awarded when a legal injury is suffered but there is no substantial loss or injury to be compensated" (*Black's Law Dictionary*, 10th ed at 473).

necessary, and the wrongs are considered to be actionable *per se*. Would or should contemporary courts faced with a claim for *Charter* damages follow the common law and provide money compensation for violation of *Charter* provisions without the need for the plaintiff to prove consequential damages of any type or degree? If so, would the compensation be limited to nominal damages, or should the damages be more substantial in *Charter* cases?

The common law justified an award of nominal damages on the basis that it gave legal recognition to the existence of the rights infringed and served, perhaps, to provide a deterrent to others and restrain possible future breaches.[5] In addition to giving legal recognition to these early protected rights and interests, the common law also had the equally important, but not necessarily declared, purpose of trying to limit or prevent self-help by victims acting in retaliation. When faced with an actionable *per se* situation involving the *Charter*, courts theoretically could award punitive or exemplary damages as well as nominal damages "even in cases where the plaintiff could not prove or be presumed in law to have suffered any damages."[6] Given that the dignity and worth of human beings is the raison d'être of many *Charter* rights, what value, if any, should be placed on any lessening of that worth by a *Charter* violation that caused no other discernible injury? It might be argued, in opposition to any monetary remedy, that a court declaration of a *Charter* violation would provide sufficient recognition of the value and importance of the right violated without any need to compensate the victim as well.

Decisions of Canadian courts in the early years following the enactment of the *Charter* reveal conflicting approaches. In *Lagiorgia v Canada*, the trial judge responded to the suggestion by plaintiff's counsel that an unconstitutional seizure of goods automatically gave rise to damages by noting that "[o]n reading this provision [section 24(1)] I do not see any principle establishing automatic entitlement to a pecuniary remedy."[7] By contrast, one year later, the British Columbia court in *Lord v Allison* awarded the plaintiff not only compensatory damages of $3,500 and punitive damages of $1,500 but also $1,000 for violation of his *Charter* rights. The court declared that "there should be an appropriate award for the infringement

5 See *The Mediana*, [1900] AC 113 at 116, Halsbury L.

6 Ken Cooper-Stephenson, *Charter Damages Claims* (Toronto: Carswell, 1990) at 239.

7 (1985), 18 CRR 348 at 355 (FCTD), rev'd in part [1987] 3 FC 28 (CA), leave to appeal to SCC refused (1988), 61 CR (3d) xxviii.

alone, regardless of common law principles relating to damages."[8] Although the remarks of the British Columbia court were made in the narrow context of the question of automatic entitlement to compensation for any *Charter* violation, they are equally relevant to the broader question of common law damages principles as a basis for *Charter* damages. Should common law damages principles be the basis or model for *Charter* damages or only a useful guide? This question is relevant both to the narrow issue of automatic entitlement to damages for any *Charter* violation and to the broader issue of the concept or scope of consequential losses or harm.

C. DIFFERENT LOSS SCENARIOS AND THE COMMON LAW RESPONSE

At common law, the onus is on the plaintiff to prove the damages suffered, but this onus may be faced in a number of different situations. In the first and most straightforward case, the plaintiff has suffered real losses of a type that the law recognizes and has sufficient factual evidence to prove the loss. In such circumstances, the onus can be met without difficulty, and the court will award monetary compensation. In the second scenario, the plaintiff has again suffered real, legally recognized losses or harm but lacks the necessary factual evidence to prove the loss. In this situation, and in some cases such as libel and slander, the law assists the plaintiff by presuming that losses have occurred. Damages are declared by the court to be "at large."[9] In a third situation, the plaintiff has suffered a real loss, but it is not of a type that the law recognizes as worthy of a compensatory remedy. Some forms of economic loss deemed too indirect and too remote, for example, are not compensated by the common law rules of damages. Similarly, types of emotional trauma such as distress, humiliation, and anxiety if not serious enough to qualify as a recognized psychological injury are not compensated. They may be described as consequential losses, harms, or injuries, but the common law will not compensate the plaintiff for them.[10] The final

---

8 (1986), 3 BCLR (2d) 300 at 316 (SC). The court awarded $500 for violation of s 10(b) and $500 for violation of s 12 of the *Charter*.

9 See Stephen M Waddams, *The Law of Damages* (Toronto: Canada Law Book, 1991) (loose-leaf November 2014 supplement) § 1380 at 614.

10 Consequential losses are considered in law to be indirect rather than direct, but they are still recoverable in tort law if reasonably foreseeable. However, for policy reasons, emotional disturbances not severe enough to qualify as legally recognized psychological injuries are not usually compensable as tort damages.

situation involves the infringement of a right that does not cause loss or harm of any type and is designated as *damnum sine injuria*.[11] As already discussed, the common law does offer nominal damages as compensation in a limited number of situations for the purpose of recognizing and affirming legal rights.

Most instances of *Charter* violation involve either tortious acts by the defendant, with some degree of fault, or acts that are not tortious but can be considered obnoxious in terms of behaviour. Like fault, obnoxious behaviour can vary from being merely discourteous or unsympathetic to being high-handed and truly egregious. Courts in *Charter* cases seem to reserve the term "egregious" to describe conduct that is more flagrant because it is presumed to cause the plaintiff some degree of emotional trauma. Conduct that is less than egregious but still obnoxious or demeaning can still cause the victim some degree of emotional disturbance, whether distress, anxiety, or embarrassment. In *Charter* cases, courts have usually taken these consequences into account when deciding whether to award damages or not and what the amount should be. In situations lacking either fault or egregious or obnoxious behaviour on the part of the defendant, the court is faced with a bare technical violation of the *Charter.* As already noted,[12] the common law takes a very cautious approach to emotional shock or trauma that does not meet the threshold test of a recognized psychiatric illness. As one legal commentator describes it, the common law "usually lumps together emotional distress or any kind of psychological impact on the plaintiff as a single 'type' of damage, and such damage is often disallowed when it stands alone. One principal reason for this is that damage of this nature is considered part of the daily functioning of life."[13] Like libel and slander, *Charter* violations involving sections 7, 8, 9, or 12 are likely to result in some degree of emotional upset on the part of the claimant. The common law position with regard to emotional distress or trauma, if used as a guide in *Charter* cases, would limit the range or scope of consequential or presumed damages.

The common law does take into account the conduct of the defendant when assessing common law damages. If the facts establish aggressive or egregious behaviour on the part of the defendant while committing a tortious act, the court can add aggravated damages to any compensation

---

11 Use of this term by a court signifies that a legal wrong has been committed but that no legally recognized injury has resulted.

12 See discussion of the third situation or scenario at note 10, above, and accompanying text.

13 Cooper-Stephenson, above note 6 at 246.

award.[14] The impact of the defendant's behaviour upon the plaintiff is also a factor in awarding aggravated damages. In this way, the common law compensates the plaintiff for emotional trauma that standing alone would not merit compensation, but the defendant's conduct must be egregious. If the defendant's conduct is egregious enough to warrant punishment, punitive or exemplary damages can also be awarded by the court to punish the wrongdoer and to deter other potential wrongdoers. Both aggravated and punitive damages are awarded at common law in addition to any compensatory damages that can be proven.

D. A LIMITED ROLE FOR *PER SE* DAMAGES?

If courts were to limit the definition or scope of damages *per se* in *Charter* cases to only those situations where (1) there is no actual loss or harm in its broadest sense suffered by the victim, that is, no emotional trauma; (2) the defendant's conduct cannot be considered either tortious or egregious; and (3) there is no need to punish the defendant or to deter others, there would be very few situations left to be covered by the concept of damages *per se*. The only reason for awarding damages in situations involving none of the above-mentioned factors would be for the courts to demonstrate vindication of the *Charter* right, and perhaps some general element of deterrence. Such cases would result not in a merely nominal award, as would be the situation at common law in non-*Charter* cases, or a conventional award but, rather, an amount that the court considers to be appropriate and just in the circumstances. Very few of the *Charter* damages cases surveyed in this book would qualify for damages *per se* on the basis of the restrictive criteria enumerated above. Obviously a common judicial understanding of the rationale for awarding damages *per se* in *Charter* situations is necessary and desirable if these awards are going to make any sense. The question is, do the cases surveyed show such an understanding?

During the first eleven years after the enactment of the *Charter*, there was only one case that would fall within the restrictive definition of damages *per se*. That was the case of *Lord v Allison*,[15] in which the court awarded $3,500 in compensatory damages and a supplementary award of $1,000 for

---

14 As discussed previously in Chapter 3, Section H(2)(e)(ii). Aggravated damages are intended to soothe a plaintiff whose feelings have "been wounded by the quality of the defendant's misbehaviour": Kenneth D Cooper-Stephenson & Iwan B Saunders, *Personal Injury Damages in Canada* (Toronto: Carswell, 1981) at 55.

15 Above note 8.

violation of *Charter* sections 10(b) and 12. The trial judge gave no explanation of the basis for this award or how he reached the amount of $1,000. One case out of eight decisions in which damages were awarded represents a 13 percent *per se* damages usage rate.

In the second period of review, 1995 to 2010, there are four cases excluding *Ward v Vancouver (City)*[16] that, at first glance, seem to involve a judicial award of *per se* damages.[17] However, upon closer examination, only one case is found to be an example of damages *per se* actually being awarded in a situation where there are no consequential injuries of any sort and where the conduct of the defendant is not an issue.[18]

In the first of the four cases, *Hawley v Bapoo*, the trial judge concluded that an award of damages *per se* was not possible given the declaration of the Supreme Court of Canada in *RJR – MacDonald Inc v Canada (AG)* that "damages are not the primary remedy in *Charter* cases."[19] Fortunately, the victim in this case had also suffered consequential emotional trauma that allowed the judge to award him $2,500 in compensatory damages against each of the two defendants. In the second case, *Auton (Guardian ad litem of) v British Columbia (Minister of Health)*, the trial judge awarded the four adult petitioners $20,000 each as symbolic damages because it was not possible to award the full cost of past medical treatment.[20] This award appears to be a combination of compensation for past economic loss and vindication of *Charter* rights. However, there is no way to tell whether a portion of the award represents damages *per se* or vindication of the *Charter* right violated. In the third case, *Dulude v Canada*, the common law tort of false imprisonment and arrest had been committed, and the court noted that at common law no damages had to be proven.[21] However, the court also noted that the victim and his family had suffered anxiety, frustration, and anguish while seeking legal vindication of his *Charter* right under section 9 to be free from arbitrary detention or imprisonment. Interestingly enough, the emotional trauma recognized by the court was not the direct consequence of the

16 2007 BCSC 3, aff'd 2009 BCCA 23, var'd (*sub nom Vancouver (City) v Ward*) 2010 SCC 27 [*Ward*].

17 *Dulude v Canada* (1997), 138 FTR 301 (TD), rev'd [2000] 1 FC 545 (CA) [*Dulude*]; *Auton (Guardian ad litem of) v British Columbia (Minister of Health)*, 2001 BCSC 220, var'd 2002 BCCA 538, rev'd 2004 SCC 78 [*Auton*]; *Morin v Prince Edward Island Regional Administrative Unit #3 School Board*, 2004 PESCTD 1, var'd 2005 PESCAD 14 [*Morin*]; *Bapoo*, above note 2.

18 See *Morin*, *ibid*.

19 [1994] 1 SCR 311 at 341, quoted in *Bapoo*, above note 2 at para 204.

20 Above note 17.

21 Above note 17.

Charter violation but part of the victim's legal effort to seek vindication and recognition of the right infringed. Considering the fault of the defendant, as represented by tortious acts, and the somewhat indirect emotional impact on the victim, this case can hardly be pointed to as an example of damages *per se*.

This leaves the final case, *Morin v Prince Edward Island Regional Administrative Unit #3 School Board*, in which the trial judge awarded $15,000 for *Charter* infringement.[22] In this case, there was no fault or other egregious conduct attributed to the defendant or consequential emotional distress suffered by the victim, nor did there appear to be any judicial desire to punish the defendant. There were in fact real economic losses, but they were not recognized by the trial judge, so the $15,000 appears to have been for *Charter* violations only. The Court of Appeal did recognize that the plaintiff had suffered real economic losses and so increased the damages to $75,000.[23] This award is presumably composed of the original $15,000 damages *per se* and $60,000 for real pecuniary loss. The *Morin* case appears to be the only example before the *Ward* decision of an award of damages *per se* in the second review period. This represents only 6 percent of the sixteen cases excluding *Ward* in which *Charter* damages were awarded, compared to 13 percent in the first review period.

In *Ward*,[24] the main issue was the need for fault on the part of the defendants to support a damages award. This issue did not involve damages *per se*. However, the damages awarded to the victim because of the unreasonable seizure of his car, which constituted one head of damages, could be looked upon as an example of damages *per se* being awarded by the court. The victim alleged that the tort of conversion had been committed, but the trial judge made no mention of such tortious act when he awarded the plaintiff $100 for what he described as unreasonable search and seizure that represented a violation of section 8 of the *Charter*.[25] By describing the award of $100 as nominal damages and noting that no substantial damages had been suffered, the court seems to be equating the situation in *Ward* with the common law situation where a tort is committed and where the court wishes to recognize the infringement of the protected legal right or interest. The trial judge does not use the term "damages *per se*" as such, but in the absence of judicially recognized tortious conduct, this would seem to be an example

22 Above note 17.

23 2005 PESCAD 14.

24 *Ward*, above note 16.

25 *Ibid* at paras 92 & 93, Tysoe J.

of such an award. When the case reached the Court of Appeal,[26] that court noted that the trial judge had not considered the conversion allegation and so declined to do so unless the appeal was successful, which it was not.

Over the entire period from 1984 to 2010, there were only two cases in which the courts awarded automatic or *per se* damages: *Lord v Allison*[27] and *Morin*.[28] Additionally, there were four cases, including *Ward*, that had the potential for a *per se* damages award but in which *per se* damages were not clearly identified.[29] So courts awarded *per se* damages in 8 percent of cases in which *Charter* damages were awarded while an additional 16 percent of such cases had the potential for a *per se* damages award. It is significant that the courts offered little or no discussion of the rationale for an award of damages *per se* in *Charter* cases generally.

If courts in *Charter* cases continue to adopt a more liberal view of consequential damages, particularly in relation to emotional upset or trauma, there will be relatively few cases where one could say that there was a *Charter* violation but no loss or injury of any kind suffered by the victim, in other words a true actionable *per se* situation. This would not relieve the judiciary of the task of deciding what the appropriate remedy should be for technical violations of the *Charter*. The positive value of affirming and vindicating *Charter* rights could still justify an award of damages larger than the traditional common law award of nominal compensation. Given the wording of section 24(1), "appropriate and just in the circumstances," a conventional award seems unlikely.

E. THE ROLE OF COMMON LAW DAMAGES: PRE-*WARD* CONCLUSIONS

As to the more general question regarding the proper role for common law damages principles in guiding the development of *Charter* damages, in light of the restrictions described in Section C, above in this chapter, it would

26 2009 BCCA 23.

27 Above note 8.

28 *Morin*, above note 17.

29 The Supreme Court did not specifically address the issue of damages *per se* in *Vancouver (City) v Ward*, 2010 SCC 27. This issue as it might be affected by the new analytical framework put forth by the Court in *Ward* and the proposed functional approach to *Charter* damages is discussed briefly in Chapter 6, Section C(2). The other three cases are *Bapoo*, above note 2, *Auton*, above note 17, and *Dulude*, above note 17.

seem preferable to employ common law damages principles as a guide rather than a mandatory model to be followed exactly.[30]

30 Linden suggests that tort law "should be allowed to help" in the evolution of the new *Charter* damages jurisprudence since "tort law's central mission is to provide civil redress for wrongful conduct," and *Charter* damages are a civil remedy. Classifying these new civil actions for *Charter* damages as "constitutional torts" would, in Linden's opinion, "maintain a link to the fully developed field of tort law which would give some stability and guidance to the judges administering this new area while recognizing its public nature": Allen M Linden, "*Charter* Damage Claims: New Dawn or Mirage?" (2012) 39:4 *The Advocates' Quarterly* 426 at 430.

Chapter 6

Vancouver (City) v Ward

An Evolutionary Milestone?

A. INTRODUCTION

The latest, and perhaps the most important, stage in the evolution of *Canadian Charter of Rights and Freedoms*[1] damages as a constitutional remedy occurred in 2010 with the decision of the Supreme Court of Canada in *Vancouver (City) v Ward.*[2] In this case, the Court was required to address the question of "when damages may be awarded under s. 24(1) of the *Charter*, and what the amount of such damages should be."[3] A decision of a unanimous Court, written by McLachlin CJ, it represents a major milestone in our understanding of the nature and purpose of *Charter* damages.[4] Additionally, the decision provides an analytical framework for lower courts faced with claims for compensation for *Charter* violations.

The factual situation in *Ward* involved the detention and arrest of a Vancouver lawyer suspected of planning to throw a pie at the prime minister. The police, acting upon information describing the suspected potential

---

1 Part I of the *Constitution Act, 1982*, being Schedule B to the *Canada Act 1982* (UK), 1982, c 11 [*Charter*].

2 2010 SCC 27 [*Ward*].

3 *Ibid* at para 3.

4 Linden describes the *Ward* decision as a significant development that ranks as "a historic milestone for Charter litigation" and one that is "a welcome, comforting, needed, overdue, but I must say largely symbolic advance in our legal system." In his opinion, the decision is "a charming ornament in an already well-developed civil justice and Charter world, gently enhancing to some degree the accountability of government for Charter breaches": Allen M Linden, "*Charter* Damage Claims: New Dawn or Mirage?" (2012) 39:4 *The Advocates' Quarterly* 426 at 438 & 439.

pie thrower, arrested Mr Ward for breach of the peace when he became loud and aggressive during questioning. He was held in police custody pending further investigation, and while in detention, he was strip-searched, and his car was seized. Upon release, Mr Ward sued the city police and the province for violation of his *Charter* rights under sections 7, 8, and 9. He alleged wrongful detention, unreasonable strip search, and wrongful seizure of his car, actions that he claimed were tortious.

An examination of the trial court,[5] British Columbia Court of Appeal,[6] and Supreme Court decisions shows a considerable uniformity of result but with some differences. All three courts agreed that *Charter* damages in the amount of $5,000 were warranted for the unreasonable strip search. As for the claim of wrongful imprisonment, the trial judge and the Court of Appeal agreed that an award of an additional $5,000 was appropriate. However, this particular head of damages was not part of the appeal to the Supreme Court.[7] The trial judge also awarded Mr Ward $100 as compensation for the wrongful seizure of his car. This award was upheld by the Court of Appeal but rejected by the Supreme Court. Chief Justice McLachlin explained that a declaration of *Charter* violation was sufficient to vindicate the *Charter* right involved and to deter similar future conduct.[8] Counsel for the Crown had argued that damages should not be awarded for *Charter* violations not involving tortious acts, citing the Ontario Court of Appeal decision in *Wynberg v Ontario*.[9]

B. A NEW ANALYTICAL FRAMEWORK

In reaching its conclusions in *Ward*, the Supreme Court of Canada employed a new analytical framework to determine whether *Charter* damages were an appropriate and just remedy and the quantum of damages. This development, coming perhaps in response to the most recent plea for such a framework from Saunders J, dissenting, in the Court of Appeal in *Ward*,[10] as well as the many earlier observations and expressed desires for such Supreme Court direction from other lower courts, represents the most important part of the *Ward* decision. As described by McLachlin CJ, the analytical framework involves six considerations or issues that are relevant to the ap-

5 *Ward v Vancouver (City)*, 2007 BCSC 3, Tysoe J [*Ward* SC].
6 *Ward v Vancouver (City)*, 2009 BCCA 23, aff'g 2007 BCSC 3 [*Ward* CA].
7 *Ward*, above note 2 at para 11.
8 *Ibid* at para 78.
9 (2006), 82 OR (3d) 561 (CA).
10 *Ward* CA, above note 6 at para 83.

plication of section 24(1) and to the question whether damages are available under that section as a *Charter* remedy.[11] The six considerations or issues to be kept in mind by the courts are as follows:

1) the language of section 24(1) and the nature of *Charter* damages
2) whether a *Charter* right has been violated and a breach of *Charter* provisions committed
3) whether damages are an appropriate and just remedy, as determined by having regard to whether they would fulfill one or more of the stated functions of the remedy, namely, compensation, vindication of the right, and deterrence of future breaches
4) whether the state can establish countervailing factors that would defeat the functional considerations and thus render damages inappropriate or unjust as a *Charter* remedy
5) what would be an appropriate and just assessment of the quantum of damages
6) whether the court has jurisdiction to award *Charter* damages and what procedure the court should adopt when the plaintiff claims both tort damages and *Charter* damages

Considerations one and six are directed at more general issues, such as the proper approach to the interpretation of section 24(1) to determine whether *Charter* damages can be awarded as a *Charter* remedy (consideration one) and whether the court has the necessary jurisdiction to supply such a remedy (consideration six). Considerations two, three, four, and five, on the other hand, address more specifically the issue of state liability. The Chief Justice refers to each of these latter considerations as a "step" in the process of determining whether *Charter* damages are an appropriate and just remedy.[12] They can be presented in the following abbreviated form:

Step one: proof of *Charter* breach
Step two: purposes of *Charter* damages — functional approach[13]
Step three: countervailing factors
Step four: quantum of damages — functional approach

This four-step process has become the touchstone test used by later courts to determine state liability when faced with claims for *Charter* damages.

With regard to the presentation of evidence at trial, the claimant has the initial burden of establishing that an award of *Charter* damages is an

11 *Ward*, above note 2 at para 15.
12 *Ibid* at para 4.
13 See *ibid* at paras 24 and 32.

appropriate and just remedy, applying the functional approach of step two. If the claim passes this functional test, a *prima facie* claim is made out, and the evidentiary onus then shifts to the defendant to negate the *prima facie* award claim by producing countervailing considerations, such as alternative remedies or good governance concerns (step three). The court must then weigh the *prima facie* case against the countervailing factors to determine whether an award should be made and, if so, assess what the quantum will be (step four).[14]

In the context of the factual situation in *Ward*, the Supreme Court was required to deal with only two claims of *Charter* violation even though several other violations had been asserted by the claimant and dealt with by the lower courts.[15] The two claims before the Supreme Court involved the strip search of Mr Ward at the police station and the seizure of his car. In dealing with the strip search, Tysoe J, the trial judge, found that the corrections officers had violated Mr Ward's *Charter* rights under section 8. The defendants did not challenge this finding before the Supreme Court, and the Court simply accepted Tysoe J's findings on this issue.

An examination of Tysoe J's reasons for concluding that the strip search constituted a breach of section 8 reveals that he considered the strip search to be unreasonable. He reached this conclusion because, in his opinion, Mr Ward presented no danger to the safety and security of the jail at the time of the search and because the search had not been conducted in accordance with corrections branch written policy.[16] He further found that the failure to comply with the strip search policy had not been deliberate. On the contrary, the two officers involved had not known that "it was wrong to continue imprisoning Mr. Ward after the Prime Minister left the area . . . ."[17] An unreasonable search in this particular context appears to mean one that is unnecessary, that may or may not have been prompted by improper motives, and that does not intentionally breach institutional policy or protocol. Justice Tysoe makes no specific mention of fault as an element of *Charter* breach: he neither suggests it as a necessary element of proving breach nor denies it as a requirement. However, the fact that the breach of institutional

14 See *ibid* at paras 35 and 45.

15 The factual situation in *Ward*, *ibid*, can be analyzed in terms of five separate instances of potential *Charter* breach and violation of *Charter* rights: (1) the initial detention and handcuffing of Mr Ward, (2) the initial detention or arrest of Mr Ward at the police station, (3) the continued detention and court-determined arrest of Mr Ward at the police station, (4) the strip search of Mr Ward, and (5) the seizure of Mr Ward's car.

16 *Ward* SC, above note 5 at para 86.

17 *Ibid* at para 104.

policy was inadvertent could be interpreted as an indication that fault, in this situation, was not required.

The second claim before the Supreme Court involved the seizure of Mr Ward's car. Mr Ward alleged that the wrongful seizure of his property constituted the civil tort of conversion. Justice Tysoe found the seizure to be wrongful, which presumably means that the seizure had been unjustified. However, in his decision, Tysoe J did not deal with the tort claim as such.[18] Perhaps he thought that Mr Ward had not been deprived of his property long enough for the seizure to constitute the tort of conversion. Although not tortious, the wrongful seizure of the car did amount to a breach of Mr Ward's *Charter* rights, a breach that warranted a *Charter* damages award of $100.

Since the damages award of $100 had not been contested before the Supreme Court, Canada's highest court accepted the finding of Tysoe J as to the issue of breach without comment. However, with regard to the remedy provided by the trial judge (i.e., *Charter* damages of $100), the Supreme Court was of the view that a declaration would be the more appropriate and just remedy. In the Court's opinion, this remedy would be sufficient to meet the need for vindication of the right protected by section 8 of the *Charter* and to deter future improper car seizures.[19] Insofar as fault is concerned, the Supreme Court could be viewed as taking the position that wrongful, but not tortious, conduct is sufficient to meet the breach requirement in the analytical framework.

By simply accepting the findings of the trial judge on both of these issues without any comment, the Supreme Court did little to clarify the question whether fault has any role to play in the court's determination of breach.

C. THE NEW FRAMEWORK AS APPLIED TO *WARD*

The application of this analytical framework to the facts of *Ward* produces the following explanation of the results.

1) $5,000 for the Unreasonable Strip Search[20]

As McLachlin CJ explained, compensation was necessary because of what she described as the "egregious" conduct of the police and the serious effect

18 See *Ward* SC, above note 5 at paras 92 & 93.

19 *Ward*, above note 2 at para 78.

20 For a discussion of this issue, see *ibid* at paras 61–66.

it had upon Mr Ward.[21] The effect referred to was the humiliation produced by the strip search. As McLachlin CJ emphasized, strip searches, regardless of the way in which they are conducted, are inherently degrading and humiliating and "constitute significant injury to an individual's intangible interests . . . ."[22] Such effects may not produce psychological or emotional distress significant enough to support a court claim for intentional infliction of emotional shock but nevertheless have a serious impact upon the person's dignity that, in the constitutional context, is compensable. This approach seems to answer the concerns that some lower courts had expressed about providing *Charter* damages when there was no real injury in the sense understood by tort law. Insofar as other functions of *Charter* damages are concerned, the Chief Justice considered the police conduct to require that the vindication and deterrent functions be satisfied by a damages award.[23] Addressing the question of quantum, the Chief Justice noted that the strip search had been relatively brief, had not been extremely disrespectful, and had involved no touching or consequential physical or psychological injury.[24] The officers' conduct was not intentional, malicious, high-handed, or oppressive although it was insensitive to *Charter* rights.[25] The plaintiff's injury, she suggested, was serious but not at the high end of seriousness. Presumably, this means moderately serious. All of the above considerations pointed to a modest award that was the amount awarded by the trial judge. It is worth noting that, according to McLachlin CJ, subjecting a person to a strip search amounts to egregious conduct. Additional disrespectful action is not required. The reason, as the Chief Justice explained, is that strip searches are inherently degrading and humiliating and have a significant impact by themselves on a person's dignity.[26]

As far as countervailing factors were concerned, McLachlin CJ noted that other remedies, such as tort remedies, were not available and that a declaration would not be sufficient.[27] The Chief Justice concluded that the state had failed to show that the Court's *prima facie* conclusion that a damages award for the strip search was both appropriate and just in the circumstances was negated by good governance considerations, such as those

21 *Ibid* at para 64.
22 *Ibid*.
23 *Ibid* at para 66.
24 *Ibid* at para 71.
25 *Ibid* at para 72.
26 *Ibid* at para 64.
27 *Ibid* at para 68.

raised in *Mackin v New Brunswick (Minister of Finance)*.[28] The award was not unfair to the state.

2) No Damages for the Car Seizure[29]

Applying the new functional approach to the car seizure, the Supreme Court found that compensation was not necessary because, while Mr Ward's *Charter* rights had been violated and while the acts of the police had been wrong, he did not suffer any injury as a result of the violation.[30] Chief Justice McLachlin noted that although the car had been moved (towed to the police compound), it had not been searched because the police did not have the necessary warrant. The Chief Justice further noted that the police conduct after the seizure had been accommodating rather than disrespectful or unhelpful, making punishment unnecessary. As to the effect of the seizure upon Mr Ward, McLachlin CJ pointed out that there had been no illegal search of the car and that he had been deprived of the use of his car for only a short time. Presumably, this short loss of use was not considered to be serious enough in the eyes of the Court to qualify or support a claim for conversion although Mr Ward's counsel had alleged such a tortious act. Finally, although the Court did not specifically say so, the effect of the wrongful seizure of the car on Mr Ward's dignity was not significant enough to warrant compensation.

The facts as described above appear to have convinced the Supreme Court that there was no need to vindicate Mr Ward's *Charter* right or to deter future wrongful conduct beyond a declaration of *Charter* violation, and so the trial award of $100 was overturned.[31] The issue of damages *per se* was not directly or specifically mentioned by the Supreme Court, but this situation, if correctly viewed as involving no tort of conversion, would appear to fit the criteria for such an award as illustrated by decisions preceding *Ward* and discussed in Chapter 5, Section D. Application of the functional approach places the emphasis on functionality and would appear to spell the demise of *per se* damages in *Charter* cases. Or perhaps the Supreme Court thought that the vindication of *Charter* rights was sufficiently achieved in this specific case by the award of money compensation ($5,000) for the unreasonable strip search and detention.

---

28 2002 SCC 13 [*Mackin*].

29 For a discussion of this issue, see *Ward*, above note 2 at paras 74–78.

30 *Ibid* at para 77.

31 To use the Court's words, *ibid*, "The object of compensation is not engaged by the seizure of the car."

D. THE FUNCTIONAL APPROACH TO DAMAGES

In addition to its proposed analytical framework for determining when damages are available under section 24(1), the Supreme Court of Canada also advocated a functional approach to or justification for damages awards. As McLachlin CJ explained, a "functional approach to damages finds damages to be appropriate and just to the extent that they serve a useful function or purpose."[32] One general useful purpose according to the Chief Justice is advancing the general objectives of the *Charter*.[33] A damages award can do this in three interrelated ways: first, by compensating the claimant for any personal loss that may have resulted from the *Charter* breach; second, by emphasizing the importance of the *Charter* rights and the fact that they "must be maintained, and cannot be allowed to be whittled away by attrition"[34] — the function or purpose of vindicating *Charter* rights; and third, by deterring, it is hoped, future breaches of the *Charter* by state actors — the function of deterrence.[35] The Chief Justice explained that to meet the appropriate and just requirements of section 24(1), the claimant must demonstrate that a damages award would achieve one or more of these objectives.[36]

1) Compensation

Described as the most important purpose of damages awards, compensation recognizes that a breach of *Charter* rights may cause individuals personal loss. This loss should be compensated, and the claimant put in the position he would have been in if the *Charter* had not been breached. This goal of public law damages seems to be the same as that of private law damages, that is, *restitutio in integrum*, except for the fact that public law compensation is broader. According to McLachlin CJ, personal loss or losses are composed of four elements: (1) physical harm, (2) psychological harm (serious), (3) pecuniary loss, and (4) intangible loss.[37] The last is unique to public law in that it covers personal emotional reactions such as humiliation, embarrassment, and anxiety, none of which would be considered legally recognized injuries in private or civil law. In many cases, these emotional reactions are incorporated or subsumed in psychological injury of a more serious type. But in cases where they are not, they should be recognized as

32 *Ibid* at para 24.
33 *Ibid* at para 25.
34 *Ibid.*
35 *Ibid.*
36 *Ibid* at para 31.
37 *Ibid* at para 27.

compensable independent injuries, according to McLachlin CJ, even though they are very difficult to measure.[38]

There is another level of emotional reaction or loss that is even further removed from a legally recognized psychological injury or a more intangible interest like humiliation or embarrassment. This emotional response involves disappointment that *Charter* rights have not been respected or perhaps anger at the violation. In some cases where the violation has been ongoing, there may be severe frustration as in the case of *Auton (Guardian ad litem of) v British Columbia (Minister of Health)*.[39] Whether such a less serious emotional reaction should be compensated or left to be recognized under other damages functions like vindication or deterrence is an open question at this stage. As a final observation, the emotional response to an egregious tortious act is usually taken into account by the awarding of aggravated damages, but the *Ward* decision makes no reference to this type of compensation.

2) Vindication

As the Chief Justice explained, vindication, a second function of damages awards, serves to affirm constitutional values and has been "recognized as a valid object of damages in many jurisdictions."[40] Acknowledged as providing support for the compensation function, vindication recognizes that *Charter* rights must be maintained and not be allowed to be diminished. It emphasizes the importance of *Charter* rights and focuses on the harm to society as the primary harm. Vindication is deemed necessary because of the perceived danger that violation of *Charter* rights if allowed to go unchallenged would erode public confidence and diminish public faith in the efficacy of constitutional protection. In this sense, there is a deterrent aspect to vindication damages.

3) Deterrence

As an objective of *Charter* damages, deterrence "is not aimed at deterring the specific wrongdoer, but rather at influencing government behaviour in order to secure state compliance with the *Charter* in the future."[41] In this sense,

38 *Ibid*. As McLachlin CJ explained, *ibid*, "a resilient claimant whose intangible interests are harmed should not be precluded from recovering damages simply because she cannot prove a substantial psychological injury."

39 2001 BCSC 220, var'd 2002 BCCA 538, rev'd 2004 SCC 78.

40 *Ward*, above note 2 at para 28.

41 *Ibid* at para 29.

deterrence is similar to the criminal sentencing objective of general deterrence. The objective or purpose of deterrence, like vindication, has been widely recognized by the international community according to the Chief Justice.[42] Deterrence, together with vindication, "will support the compensatory function and bolster the appropriateness of an award of damages."[43]

E. AN ELABORATION OF THE ANALYTICAL FRAMEWORK

Following her brief outline of the six considerations that compose the suggested analytical framework,[44] McLachlin CJ provided a more detailed discussion of several of the considerations. Her first remarks concerned the language of section 24(1) and the nature of *Charter* damages. Drawing upon comments by other members of the Supreme Court of Canada in earlier cases, McLachlin CJ observed that the language of section 24(1) is broad and confers upon courts a wide discretion.[45] At the same time, she cautioned courts, and appellate courts in particular, not to reduce this wide discretion by surrounding it with judicially prescribed conditions.[46] What these conditions may be are not revealed in the judgment, but it is possible that one example may be a requirement that the defendant exhibit a particular state of mind as a prerequisite to an award of *Charter* damages. Alternatively, the reference may have been to any attempt by the courts to develop some sort of binding formula that would be applied to all cases regardless of specific circumstances in an individual case.

However, judicial clarification as to when it may be "appropriate and just" to award damages is permissible, according to the Chief Justice, particularly in light of the fact that this phrase places limits on what remedies are available.[47] Just what those limits are will be determined by the facts and circumstances of the particular case with guidance provided by decisions in prior cases. Chief Justice McLachlin acknowledged that the Supreme

42 Citing, *ibid* at paras 28 & 29, *Fose v Minister of Safety and Security*, 1997 (3) S Afr LR 786 at para 55 (Const Ct); *AG of Trinidad and Tobago v Ramanoop*, [2005] UKPC 15 at para 19; *Taunoa v AG*, [2007] NZSC 70 at para 259; *Smith v Wade*, 461 US 30 at 49 (1983).

43 *Ward*, above note 2 at para 30.

44 *Ibid* at para 15.

45 *Ibid* at para 17.

46 The Chief Justice, *ibid* at para 18, did not specifically mention appeal courts in her caution but did quote the remarks of McIntyre J in *Mills v The Queen*, [1986] 1 SCR 863 at 965: "it is not for appellate courts to pre-empt or cut down this wide discretion."

47 *Ward*, above note 2 at para 19.

Court in *Doucet-Boudreau v Nova Scotia (Minister of Education)*[48] had set out suggested general considerations that would govern what constitutes an appropriate and just remedy.[49] Applying these considerations, McLachlin CJ concluded that section 24(1) is broad enough in its language to include the remedy of damages for *Charter* violations. However, she cautioned that damages are a new remedy and should be developed incrementally, keeping in mind that damages are only one remedy of several available under section 24, and in some cases other remedies may be more appropriate.[50]

The Court in *Ward* also emphasized that *Charter* damages are not the same as private law damages in that constitutional damages result from actions against the state directly, and not individuals. Constitutional damages are distinct in that they make the state directly and primarily liable. This is not to say that policy considerations that are relevant when a court awards private damages against state actors may not be relevant to and appropriately kept in mind by a court when considering *Charter* damages as a remedy.[51] The unspoken caveat is that such policies should not be determinative of the *Charter* remedy decision.

1) Countervailing Factors[52]

Although a plaintiff may be able to make out a *prima facie* case for *Charter* damages by satisfying the functionality test, the state can argue and try to establish that there are other factors rendering an award inappropriate or unjust. In the opinion of McLachlin CJ, as of the date of the *Ward* decision, just two considerations or factors had been established or recognized. The first was the possibility of alternative remedies that could be considered appropriate and just. The second involved concerns for good governance.[53]

a) Alternative Remedies

Alternative remedies include "private law remedies for actions for personal injury [such as torts], other *Charter* remedies like declarations under s. 24(1), and remedies for actions covered by legislation permitting proceedings against the Crown."[54] The state has to show that remedies other than damages are

48 2003 SCC 62 [*Doucet-Boudreau*].
49 *Ward*, above note 2 at para 20.
50 *Ibid* at para 21.
51 *Ibid* at para 22.
52 For the Supreme Court's general discussion of countervailing factors, see *ibid* at paras 32–45.
53 *Ibid* at para 33.
54 *Ibid* at para 34.

available in the particular case and will sufficiently address the breach of *Charter* rights.[55] The existence of a potential private law remedy, such as for a tort action, does not bar a claimant from obtaining damages under the *Charter*, but if the claimant has commenced a concurrent action in tort, "it is open to the state to argue that, should the tort claim be successful, the resulting award of damages would adequately address the *Charter* breach."[56]

b) Good Governance Concerns

The second countervailing consideration involves concerns for good governance. It can be argued that compliance with *Charter* standards is a foundation principle of good governance, but good governance concerns may take different forms. One concern is that any award under section 24(1) would have a chilling effect on government conduct and impact negatively on good governance. The Chief Justice in *Ward* rejected this argument because if accepted, no damages claims could be brought, and in her opinion this was not what Parliament had intended.[57] On the other hand, it may be argued that *Charter* damages deter *Charter* breaches and in this sense promote good governance.

Another approach that the government might take, as suggested by the Chief Justice, would be to argue that damages awards should be available only in situations where state conduct meets a minimum threshold of seriousness or gravity.[58] This qualified immunity approach argues that the state must have some immunity when it is performing certain legislative and policy-making functions that only the state can perform. In addition, there are situations where state action is taken under a statute that is later struck down.[59] In these circumstances, any such action should not give rise to public law damages because good governance requires that public officials carry out their duties under valid statutes without fear of liability if a statute is later struck down. The qualified immunity type of situation, illustrated by the case of *Mackin*,[60] may not be the only situation where the state could argue that damages would deter state agents from doing their job, but, as McLachlin CJ observed, no other situations have been established to date, although other situations may be recognized in the future.[61]

---

55 *Ibid* at para 35.

56 *Ibid.*

57 *Ibid* at para 38.

58 *Ibid* at para 39.

59 As was the case in *Mackin*, above note 28, discussed by the Chief Justice in *Ward*, above note 2 at paras 39–43.

60 *Mackin*, above note 28.

61 *Ward*, above note 2 at para 42.

As the law matures, it is quite possible that different defences to section 24(1) claims may emerge as other effective governance concerns arise in the future. Different situations may require different thresholds of liability, as is the case in private law. Chief Justice McLachlin suggested that one such threshold might be a "clear disregard for the claimant's *Charter* rights . . . ."[62]

2) Quantum of Damages[63]

The *Ward* decision makes it clear that two of the important considerations courts must keep in mind when deciding whether damages are to be awarded also apply to the determination of quantum of damages. These considerations are, first, that the amount awarded must be appropriate and just and, second, that it must be a meaningful award in the sense that it adequately recognizes, affirms, and vindicates the *Charter* rights of the claimant.[64] A meaningful award will be one that serves one or more of the functional objectives of compensation, vindication, and deterrence. A *Charter* damages award will follow or apply the private law tort principle of *restitutio in integrum*, particularly with regard to pecuniary losses, but non-pecuniary losses will also be recognized as a valid part of a *Charter* damages award.[65]

A principal guide for courts addressing the issue of quantum is the seriousness of the breach as measured by the objectives of section 24(1). Two factors are important in the assessment of how serious the breach is. One is the nature of the defendant's conduct: how egregious was it? The second factor is the impact of that conduct upon the claimant. The more egregious the conduct and the more serious the impact, the greater will be the emphasis upon vindication and deterrence, both of which will be reflected in the amount awarded.[66]

However, in cases of serious infringement of *Charter* rights, the amount awarded must be fair to both parties.[67] An excessively large amount may not be functionally useful in meeting the claimant's needs (or in vindicating the claimant's rights and deterring future state conduct). It may result in the diversion of a large amount of public money to private interests. There is also the risk that large awards will deter government from undertaking

---

62 *Ibid* at para 43.

63 For issues associated with the determination of the amount of *Charter* damages to be awarded and the approach that courts should take to determine the appropriate amount as outlined by the Chief Justice, see *ibid* at paras 46–55.

64 *Ibid* at para 47.

65 *Ibid* at paras 48–50.

66 *Ibid* at para 52.

67 *Ibid* at para 53.

beneficial new policies and programs. The assumption here appears to be that such policies would involve some risk of *Charter* infringement. So while the damages award must represent a meaningful response to the seriousness of the *Charter* breach and to the other objectives of *Charter* damages, there are limits. Chief Justice McLachlin summarized the issue of quantum in the following way:

> To sum up, the amount of damages must reflect what is required to functionally serve the objects of compensation, vindication of the right and deterrence of future breaches, insofar as they are engaged in a particular case, having regard to the impact of the breach on the claimant and the seriousness of the state conduct. The award must be appropriate and just from the perspective of the claimant and the state.[68]

This approach to damages would appear to preclude courts from establishing conventional awards or setting minimum or maximum dollar limits.

F. PRIOR ISSUES DISCUSSED IN *WARD*

The *Ward*[69] decision also dealt with prior and ongoing issues relating to *Charter* damages awards. These included the requirement of fault, qualified immunity, punitive damages, the jurisdiction of criminal courts, and, finally, concurrent tort claims. Of these, the first two issues generated the most discussion and comment by the Supreme Court of Canada.

1) The Requirement of Fault, or the Question of the Defendant's State of Mind

The thorny issue of fault as a prerequisite to *Charter* damages, which had generated so much debate in the pre-*Ward* era, lost much of its focus and importance in *Ward*, where it became subsumed under the more general functional approach. Instead of being the main factor in determining *Charter* breach, fault, under the *Ward* approach, became just one of several elements to be weighed and balanced by the court with reference to the ultimate question: are *Charter* damages an appropriate and just remedy in the situation?

In the context of the *Ward* approach, conduct that may be described as malicious, high-handed, or oppressive is still legally relevant but relevant to

68 *Ibid* at para 57.

69 *Ward*, above note 2.

the need for vindication or deterrence rather than to the question of breach of *Charter*.[70] The conduct of the corrections officers in *Ward*, particularly in relation to the strip search of Mr Ward, could be considered faulty in a broad sense because the officers did not demonstrate a suitable level of sensitivity to *Charter* rights.[71] While this was not fault in a legal or tortious sense, there was, in the opinion of the Supreme Court, some degree of fault or lack of reasonableness demonstrated by the officers' bad judgment or lack of awareness. It was this behaviour that the Court took into consideration as one element in the determination of the ultimate issue of whether Mr Ward was entitled to an appropriate and just remedy.

2) Qualified Immunity

Similarly, the contentious issue of qualified immunity as a defence and the question of its scope now falls to be considered under the broader category of countervailing factors or considerations that would render *Charter* damages inappropriate or unjust. One of these is the effect on good governance. Chief Justice McLachlin conceded that in some situations unless state conduct meets a minimum threshold of gravity involving wilful disregard of *Charter* rights or perhaps malice, the state may be able to establish that an award of *Charter* damages would interfere with good governance such that damages should not be awarded.[72] The government had argued that the *Mackin*[73] principle should be applied to the facts of *Ward*.

Chief Justice McLachlin rejected that argument, declaring that *Mackin* did not apply because there was no valid statute later declared to be invalid and because it was not a case of a duly enacted law being enforced until declared invalid.[74] In essence, the *Ward* case was about state actors improperly enforcing a valid government policy. As Low J in the Court of Appeal pointed out, this kind of situation will arise "most often in the context of detention, arrest and confinement by government agents charged with criminal investigation and public safety duties."[75] Up to the time of *Ward*, no appellate court had ruled on this situation,[76] but McLachlin CJ did,

---

70 In the words of the Chief Justice, *ibid* at para 72, "The objects of vindication and deterrence engage the seriousness of the state conduct."

71 See *ibid*.

72 *Ibid* at paras 39 and 43.

73 *Mackin*, above note 28.

74 *Ward*, above note 2 at para 41.

75 *Ward* CA, above note 6 at para 49.

76 See *ibid*.

and she ruled that the immunity defence did not apply to the facts of *Ward*.[77] She did, however, concede that in the future in non-*Mackin*-like situations, a court might very well find damages to be inappropriate "on grounds of effective governance."[78] As a matter of speculation, the Supreme Court mused that the minimum threshold test might be a clear disregard of the claimant's *Charter* rights but that the threshold could vary depending upon the particular situation. Existing private law thresholds and defences, the Court suggested, could offer guidance in this regard.[79]

3) Punitive Damages

Although punitive damages were not an issue in *Ward*, McLachlin CJ nevertheless observed that Gonthier J in *Mackin*[80] had speculated that a plaintiff could, in theory, seek both compensatory and punitive damages.[81] She also observed that in public law the punitive damages aspect is built into awards that reflect or serve the vindication and deterrence functions and that there is a general reluctance on the part of the international community to award purely punitive damages.[82] Her observation clearly reflects the viewpoint that punitive damages, as a separate head of damages, are not really required in *Charter* cases.

A review of lower-court decisions, however, suggests that up to the time of the *Ward* decision, lower courts had imposed punitive damages as part of *Charter* awards, but primarily in cases where the conduct had been egregious.[83] Presumably, as a result of the *Ward* decision, this factor will now be built into the general damages award as part of the vindication or deterrence function.

4) Tort-and-*Charter* Conflict: The Problem of Potential Double Compensation

Chief Justice McLachlin affirmed that a potential tort claim does not prevent a claimant from obtaining *Charter* damages. As she explained, tort law and the *Charter* are "distinct legal avenues" to obtaining compensation.[84]

---

77 *Ward*, above note 2 at para 41.
78 *Ibid* at para 42.
79 *Ibid* at para 43.
80 *Mackin*, above note 28.
81 *Ward*, above note 2 at para 56.
82 *Ibid*.
83 For a list of these cases from the period 1984–94, see Appendix 10.
84 *Ward*, above note 2 at para 36.

However, if the claimant succeeds in a concurrent tort action and is awarded civil damages, an action for section 24(1) *Charter* damages will be barred if the result would be double compensation.[85] The Chief Justice, therefore, suggests that if a tort claim is to be joined with a section 24(1) claim, "[i]t may be useful to consider the tort claim first, since if it meets the objects of *Charter* damages, recourse to s. 24(1) will be unnecessary."[86]

One legal commentator has interpreted the Chief Justice's remarks as having the effect that any claimant who makes a tort claim concurrent with a *Charter* claim for damages will be denied or prevented from making the *Charter* claim "whenever a court decides that tort law may provide a sufficient remedy."[87] This may be overstating the effect of McLachlin CJ's remarks in light of the fact that she also states that the "existence of a potential claim in tort does not therefore bar a claimant from obtaining damages under the *Charter*."[88] Perhaps the different interpretations result from the fact that a *Charter* claim will still be available in those cases where the tort action does not meet or fulfill all the objectives of a *Charter* claim. On the other hand, if a "sufficient remedy" is intended to include situations where the tort action meets all the objectives of a *Charter* action, there is no difference in the interpretations. In practice, many concurrent tort claims will pre-empt *Charter* claims unless the court is of the opinion that the tort award will not provide sufficient vindication of *Charter* rights or sufficient deterrence.

5) Concurrent Remedies

Although concurrent remedies were not an issue, McLachlin CJ affirmed and confirmed the ruling in *Schachter v Canada*[89] by declaring that "an action for damages under s. 24(1) of the *Charter* cannot be combined with an action for invalidity [and declaration] based on s. 52 of the *Constitution Act, 1982* . . . ."[90] She also decided that as far as the car seizure was concerned, a declaration issued under section 24(1) was a preferable remedy to damages, also available under section 24(1). The issue of concurrent remedies under section 52(1) and section 24(1) did not arise in the *Ward* case because the situation did not involve a statute that the court found to be invalid. If this

85 *Ibid.*
86 *Ibid* at para 59.
87 Linden, above note 4 at 439.
88 *Ward*, above note 2 at para 36.
89 [1992] 2 SCR 679 [*Schachter*].
90 *Ward*, above note 2 at para 39.

had been the case, a declaration of invalidity would have been issued by the court, but under the authority of section 52(1) rather than section 24(1).

G. PRIOR ISSUES NOT DISCUSSED IN *WARD*

1) Language

The issue of language and in particular the meaning of specific terms like "symbolic" or "moral damages" was not directly addressed in the *Ward*[91] decision because it was subsumed in the new discussion of the functions or purposes of *Charter* damages, particularly the purpose of vindication. Future discussions will focus not so much upon the literal meaning of the term "vindication" as upon the manner of its application. For example, in *Ward*, the lower courts thought that a damages award of $100 was needed to vindicate Mr Ward's right to not have his car unlawfully seized while McLachlin CJ thought that a declaration of Charter breach would suffice and explained why.[92] There will inevitably be differences in the exercise of judicial judgment and discretion even though the function or purpose of vindication as a component of *Charter* damages may be clearly understood by the courts.

Because the *Ward* case did not involve a jury, the Supreme Court of Canada probably saw no need to comment upon the added complexities of a jury trial in the abstract.

2) Aggravated Damages

Perhaps because they had been the subject of considerable discussion by the Nova Scotia Court of Appeal in *Bevis v CTV Inc (cob ATV/CTV)*,[93] aggravated damages were not discussed by the Supreme Court in relation to *Charter* damages under section 24(1) in the *Ward* decision. However, the Supreme Court did indicate that use of the new functional approach by a court would mean that there would be no need to designate and assess punitive damages as a separate aspect of the damages award.[94] Any punitive purpose will, in

---

91 *Ward*, above note 2.

92 It was her view that although the seizure of the car was wrong, "it was not of a serious nature" (*ibid* at para 77) and that a declaration would be sufficient to meet the need for vindication of *Charter* rights and deterrence of future improper car seizures (*ibid* at para 78).

93 2004 NSSC 247, var'd 2006 NSCA 56.

94 As the Chief Justice explained in *Ward*, above note 2 at para 56, "[t]he reality is that public law damages, in serving the objects of vindication and deterrence, may assume a punitive aspect." However, the Chief Justice also noted

the future, be satisfied by the court's consideration of the vindication and deterrence purposes of *Charter* damages. By implication and extension of this reasoning, it will no longer be necessary for courts to designate aggravated damages as a separate aspect of the damages award. The emotional impact of the defendant's conduct on the victim in terms of humiliation, embarrassment, anxiety, etc., will be accounted for in the general compensatory part of the damages award by using the new functional approach. The defendant's egregious conduct will likewise be taken into account, not as part of aggravated damages, but as part of the vindication function of *Charter* damages. As the Supreme Court cautions in *Ward*, while analogies to private law damages may be useful, that does not necessarily mean they will be adopted.[95] The elements that make up the final damages award may now have different labels, but as long as lawyers understand their purpose or purposes and how they relate to the traditional tort heads of damages, the change should not prove problematic.

H. TORT LAW AS A GUIDE TO *CHARTER* DAMAGES

The final aspect of the *Ward*[96] decision worth noting is the degree or extent to which the Supreme Court of Canada uses tort principles in dealing with the issue of quantum of damages and as an aid in determining what are appropriate and just *Charter* damages. Although beginning with the admonition that tort law and the *Charter* are "distinct legal avenues" to obtaining a damages remedy,[97] the Supreme Court nevertheless draws on tort experience for assistance as it develops the scope of the *Charter* remedy. The Court noted that particularly in the area of non-pecuniary damages, which are very difficult to measure, in personal injury cases, tort law had adopted a functional approach.[98] The Supreme Court obviously determined that a similar approach would be appropriate in determining when damages were suitable under section 24(1) of the *Charter*.

Furthermore, the Court noted that non-pecuniary losses like pain and suffering are compensable in tort law but at a fairly modest conventional rate unless there are exceptional circumstances.[99] It should be noted that

---

the general reluctance of the international community to award purely punitive damages.

95 *Ibid* at para 54.

96 *Ward*, above note 2.

97 *Ibid* at para 36.

98 *Ibid* at para 24.

99 *Ibid* at para 50.

tort law has also established a conventional award for catastrophic injury cases.[100] Pain and suffering, a non-pecuniary loss, could result from a *Charter* breach, but it is unlikely that catastrophic injuries would occur. No reference was made by the Court in *Ward* to the role that aggravated damages might play in this regard. As previously discussed, conventional awards used in tort law will probably not be used in *Charter* cases.

Tort law can also provide a useful guide to the quantum of damages that will be fair to both parties. As McLachlin CJ explained, the "private law measure of damages for similar wrongs will often be a useful guide. However, as Lord Nicholls warns in *Ramanoop*, [[2005] UKPC 15] at para. 18, 'this measure is no more than a guide because . . . the violation of the constitutional right will not always be coterminous with the cause of action at law.'"[101]

Finally, as discussed above in the context of the defence of qualified immunity,[102] private law (primarily tort law) can provide thresholds in cases where action is taken against state actors. "[E]xisting causes of action against state actors," declared McLachlin CJ, "embody a certain amount of 'practical wisdom' concerning the type of situation in which it is or is not appropriate to make an award of damages against the state."[103] It is apparent from the *Ward* decision that tort or private law principles have played, and will play, an important role in the development of *Charter* damages. The nature and purpose of damages in the private and public law contexts are different, but the extent of that difference is still being explored. Certainly there are common principles and considerations underlying both remedies though they are not identical.

I. *WARD*: CONCLUDING OBSERVATIONS

The Supreme Court of Canada's decision in *Ward*[104] is remarkable in many ways. Not only does it provide lower courts with a much-needed comprehensive analytical framework with which to work when assessing the appropriateness of claims for *Charter* damages, but the decision also tries to resolve and clarify several recurring issues relevant to the application of section 24(1).

---

100 See Chapter 3, Section H(2)(e)(i), note 109.

101 *Ward*, above note 2 at para 54.

102 See Section F(2), above in this chapter.

103 *Ward*, above note 2 at para 43.

104 *Ward*, above note 2.

Admittedly, the Supreme Court was able to draw upon several of its earlier decisions in fashioning the all-embracing decision in *Ward*. The 1994 decision in *RJR – MacDonald Inc v Canada (AG)*[105] provided direction as to the proper interpretive approach to section 24(1) while *Doucet-Boudreau*[106] outlined the underlying rationale for *Charter* damages specifically. Cases like *Schachter*[107] and *R v Demers*[108] clarified and determined the relationship between sections 52(1) and 24(1) in terms of providing *Charter* remedies generally while decisions in *Guimond v Quebec (AG)*[109] and *Mackin*[110] tried to delineate the scope of the limited or qualified immunity defence. But it was the *Ward* decision that provided not only a new analytical framework for or approach to *Charter* damages as a *Charter* remedy but also an impressive synthesis of thirty years of judicial experience with this issue.

As a result of this impressive effort, it is now possible to make with some confidence the following summary propositions:

1) *Charter* damages should be claimed against the state rather than individual state actors or officials because the state's liability is primary, not vicarious.
2) By formulating the functional approach, the Supreme Court impliedly rejected the idea of damages *per se*.
3) For the same reason, conventional awards and particularly those for intangible, non-pecuniary losses are not likely to be awarded.
4) The requirement of fault or a particular state of mind can no longer be considered the sole prerequisite to a damages award.
5) The *Mackin*[111] rule, which provides immunity to the Crown if the Crown and its officials do not act negligently, in bad faith, or in abuse of their power, does not apply to non-*Mackin*-like situations, that is, those situations not involving a statute or statutory provision.
6) Punitive damages should not be awarded as a separate head of damages to reflect the court's intention to punish the defendant or provide general deterrence.

105 [1994] 1 SCR 311.
106 *Doucet-Boudreau*, above note 48.
107 *Schachter*, above note 89.
108 2004 SCC 46.
109 [1996] 3 SCR 347 [*Guimond*].
110 *Mackin*, above note 28.
111 *Ibid*.

7) The *Schachter*[112] rule, which prohibits a court from issuing a declaration of unconstitutionality pursuant to section 52(1) and an award for *Charter* damages under section 24(1) in the same decision, except on rare occasions, is affirmed.
8) Provincial criminal courts are not courts of competent jurisdiction and therefore cannot award *Charter* damages.
9) The existence of a potential tort claim does not bar a claimant from pursuing a *Charter* claim because they are two separate and distinct legal avenues to a remedy. While a plaintiff can join a section 24(1) claim with a tort claim, it may be useful for the court to consider the tort claim first because if the tort award meets the purposes of *Charter* damages, there will be no need to go forward with the *Charter* claim. In fact, in this situation, the *Charter* claim is barred to prevent double recovery.

As the above list illustrates, the *Ward* decision addressed and tried to resolve many troublesome legal issues relevant to the awarding of *Charter* damages, but some issues still remain unresolved. For example, although the standard of fault required to avoid the limited or qualified immunity defence has been settled in *Mackin*-like situations, where an unconstitutional statute is involved, the same cannot be said of non-statute-based cases. However, McLachlin CJ did suggest that in such cases an appropriate standard or threshold for liability might be one where the claimant could show that crown officials, by their actions, had demonstrated a clear disregard for the claimant's *Charter* rights.[113] Furthermore, different situations may require different thresholds or liability standards. It seems that for non-*Mackin*-like situations the courts may apply a shifting standard.

Similarly, the role to be played by punitive damages remains unclear. Although they had been acknowledged by Gonthier J in *Guimond*[114] as a possible basis for a *Charter* damages award, McLachlin CJ in *Ward* appeared to suggest that courts may incorporate a punitive purpose when addressing the vindication and deterrence purposes of *Charter* damages.[115] Additionally, she noted the general reluctance of the international community to "award purely punitive damages" in constitutional cases.[116] A similar uncertainty remains regarding the role of aggravated damages.

A final area of continuing uncertainty remains with regard to the development and recognition by the courts of other defences besides that of

---

112 *Schachter*, above note 89.
113 *Ward*, above note 2 at para 43.
114 *Guimond*, above note 109.
115 *Ward*, above note 2 at para 56.
116 *Ibid.*

limited or qualified immunity. Such potential defences may well be recognized in the future when courts consider countervailing factors that affect good governance.[117] Only future experience with the *Ward* approach to *Charter* damages will determine whether these uncertainties are resolved.

117 *Ibid* at para 42.

Chapter 7

POST–*VANCOUVER (CITY) v WARD* RESULTS

A. INTRODUCTION

The *Vancouver (City) v Ward*[1] decision by the Supreme Court of Canada provided lower courts with a much-needed analytical structure with which to work out *Canadian Charter of Rights and Freedoms*[2] damages issues.[3] But what would be the practical effect of this decision upon *Charter* damages claims? How would potential litigants and lower courts respond to the new judicial guidance? From one commentator's perspective, the new approach appeared to be more flexible and open-ended than the pre-*Ward* judicial approach.[4] *Ward* also demonstrated that *Charter* damages, as a constitutional remedy, could serve both important public interests and personal, private needs. Damages could also fill a remedial gap in situations where a declaration of invalidity would not be considered an adequate remedy. From a more public perspective, the modest compensation awarded by the courts in *Ward* would probably not have too negative an effect on good governance.

Offsetting these positive factors are the still-existing operational restrictions on *Charter* damages, represented by jurisdictional and time limitations

---

1 2010 SCC 27, var'g (*sub nom Ward v Vancouver (City)*) 2009 BCCA 23, var'g 2007 BCSC 3 [*Ward*].

2 Part I of the *Constitution Act, 1982*, being Schedule B to the *Canada Act 1982* (UK), 1982, c 11 [*Charter*].

3 See Kent Roach, *Constitutional Remedies in Canada*, 2d ed (Toronto: Canada Law Book, 2013) (loose-leaf October 2014 supplement) § 11.400 at 11-21.

4 See *ibid*, § 11.500 at 11-26.2: in Roach's opinion, the *Ward* approach is "less rule based and restrictive than previous jurisprudence."

as well as the issue of concurrent tort claims.[5] In addition, there is a concern that the $5,000 award granted to Mr Ward might come to be considered and accepted as a conventional *Charter* award.[6] Unfortunately, post-*Ward* experience is somewhat limited, spanning only four and a half years (to the end of 2014) and involving only thirty-three cases.[7] Even so, some tentative observations can be offered.

It is interesting to note that the number of post-*Ward* cases heard by the courts per year in four and a half years, which amounts to 7.3 cases per year, is more than three times the number of cases per year for the first period, 1984–94, (1.9 per year) and more than two times the number of cases per year for the second period, 1995–2010, (3.3 per year). Greater public familiarity with the *Charter* and its remedies may account for some of the increase in the number of cases, but a more important factor may be the high-profile impact of the *Ward* decision upon the legal community. The significant increase in the number of *Charter* damages claims going to trial is even more impressive considering that during the four-and-a-half-year period, more than half a dozen claims have been rejected by the courts at the pre-trial stage due to inadequate pleadings.[8] In some of these cases, the claimants have been permitted by the court to amend their pleadings. How many of them actually re-litigated their claims is unknown.

Whether the *Ward* decision influenced the number of claims is uncertain given the relatively short time involved. But perhaps the Supreme Court's analysis of the purposes of *Charter* damages and clarification of the factors involved in establishing the proper basis for a *Charter* claim encour-

---

5 These obstacles are mentioned by Roach, *ibid*, and Allen M Linden, "*Charter* Damage Claims: New Dawn or Mirage?" (2012) 39:4 *The Advocates' Quarterly* 426. The Supreme Court in *Ward*, above note 1 at para 58, confirms that provincial criminal courts do not have the power to award damages under s 24(1) of the *Charter*.

6 See, for example, Roach, above note 3, § 11.721 at 11-31, who expresses concern that a $5,000 award might become the standard award for s 24(1) damages because of the *Ward* decision. However, he is also comforted by the fact that the Supreme Court "appears to contemplate that some higher and some lower sums will be within the range of what is appropriate and just."

7 See Appendix 1, cases 72–104.

8 *Meigs v Canada*, 2013 FC 389; *Ross v Canada* (AG), 2013 BCSC 1464; *Henry v British Columbia* (AG), 2013 BCSC 665 [*Henry* 2013 SC], rev'd 2014 BCCA 15 [*Henry* CA]; *Biladeau v Ontario* (AG), 2014 ONCA 848; *MacLellan v Canada* (AG), 2014 NSSC 280; *Mancuso v Canada (National Health and Welfare)*, 2014 FC 708; *Grann v Thunder Bay Police Services Board*, 2015 ONSC 438; *McHale v Ontario*, 2014 ONSC 5179; *Hneihen (Litigation guardian of) v Centre for Addiction and Mental Health (Queen Street Division)*, 2014 ONSC 55.

aged more victims of *Charter* violations to press their claim for a damages remedy.

B. SUCCESS RATE

While the number of claims per year may have increased post-*Ward*, the success rate has not increased. On the contrary, the success rate appears to have decreased significantly. Of the thirty-three cases in the sample, the claimants were successful in only three, for a success rate of 9 percent.[9] This compares with a pre-*Ward* success rate of 35 percent.[10] What accounts for this significant decrease in success rate? Does the new four-step liability approach of *Ward*[11] produce fewer successful claims, or does the emphasis upon the purposes of compensation, comprising step two of the analysis, result in fewer successful claims? Perhaps it is a combination of both.

Although the second step in the *Ward* liability analysis was referenced frequently by the courts in the thirty-three-case survey,[12] consideration of the purposes of *Charter* damages, as required by this step, does not appear to have been the determining factor in the rejection cases. A close reading of the thirty cases where damages claims were rejected reveals that the two most prominent reasons for rejection were (1) the claimant's failure to prove a *Charter* violation (30 percent)[13] and (2) bringing the claim against an

9 See *Elliot v Waterloo (Regional Municipality) Police Services*, 2011 ONSC 6889 [*Elliot*]; *Lamka v Waterloo (Regional Municipality) Police Services Board*, [2012] OJ No 5591 (Sm Cl Ct) [*Lamka*]; *Mason v Turner*, 2014 BCSC 211 [*Mason*].

10 For a list of these cases, see Appendix 5.

11 *Ward*, above note 1 at para 4, and paras 23–57, where the four steps are discussed in detail.

12 The second step requires a court to determine whether *Charter* damages are a just and appropriate remedy: see *ibid*.

13 See *Wiese v Martin*, 2011 SKQB 296 [*Wiese*]; *Magiskan v Thunder Bay (City) Police Services Board*, 2011 ONSC 7334 [*Magiskan*]; *Gladue v Alberta (AG)*, 2011 ABQB 651; *Hamalengwa v Bentley*, 2011 ONSC 4145 [*Hamalengwa*]; *Russell v York (Regional Municipality) Police Services Board*, 2011 ONSC 4619; *Leroux v Canada (Revenue Agency)*, 2010 BCSC 865, aff'd 2012 BCCA 63; *Brazeau v Canada (AG)*, 2012 FC 648; *VAS v Edmonton (City) Police Service*, 2014 ABQB 666; *Barton v Nova Scotia (AG)*, 2014 NSSC 192.

individual rather than the state (27 percent).[14] Countervailing factors[15] and suing a non-governmental agency[16] each accounted for 13 percent of the rejection cases. Other reasons for rejection were judicial application of a very high fault standard (three cases),[17] lack of proper court jurisdiction (three cases),[18] consent to the search (one case),[19] and potential double compensation or a tort-and-*Charter* conflict (one case).[20] In some cases, the court gave more than one reason for rejection.

C. AMOUNT OF AWARDS

Unfortunately, the number of post-*Ward*[21] cases in which *Charter* damages were awarded is only three,[22] which is quite small and makes it difficult to assess the impact of the *Ward* decision upon the quantum of *Charter* damages. The average award for these cases is $12,500, which can be compared to a pre-*Ward* average award of $21,713 if the exceptionally high awards are included or $8,633 if they are not.[23] Of the three post-*Ward* decisions, the most

14 See *Gendreau v Alberta (Department of Justice)*, 2010 ABQB 781; *Wiese*, above note 13; *Magiskan*, above note 13; *Hamalengwa*, above note 13; *Young v Ewatski*, 2012 MBCA 64, leave to appeal to SCC refused, [2012] SCCA No 440 [*Young*]; *Forrest v Ontario Provincial Police*, 2012 ONSC 429 (Div Ct) [*Forrest*]; *Mallett v McCaskill*, 2014 MBQB 227; *Adamson v Ontario*, 2014 ONSC 3787.

15 See *Vancouver (City) v Zhang*, 2010 BCCA 450, supplementary reasons 2011 BCCA 138; *DWH v DJR*, 2011 ABQB 608; *Sivia v British Columbia (Superintendent of Motor Vehicles)*, 2012 BCSC 1030, aff'd 2014 BCCA 79, aff'd (*sub nom Goodwin v British Columbia (Superintendent of Motor Vehicles)*) 2015 SCC 46; *Forrest*, above note 14.

16 See *Podolski v Cadillac Fairview Corp*, 2012 ONCJ 545; *Lobo v Carleton University*, 2012 ONSC 254, aff'd 2012 ONCA 498; *Bilich v Toronto (City) Police Services Board*, 2013 ONSC 1445 [*Bilich*]; *British Columbia Civil Liberties Assn v University of Victoria*, 2015 BCSC 39. In the *Bilich* case, the claimant incorrectly sued the police rather than the Crown.

17 See *Forrest*, above note 14; *Henry* 2013 SC, above note 8, rev'd *Henry* CA, above note 8; *Everett v McCaskill*, 2014 MBQB 185.

18 See *R v Wetzel*, 2011 SKPC 9, rev'd 2012 SKQB 24, rev'd in part 2013 SKCA 143; *Conway (Re)*, 2012 ONCA 519; *R v Reinhart*, 2012 SKQB 95.

19 See *Young*, above note 14.

20 See *Dixon v Hamilton (City) Police Services Board*, [2011] OJ No 3836 (SCJ).

21 *Ward*, above note 1.

22 See *Elliot*, above note 9; *Lamka*, above note 9; *Mason*, above note 9.

23 The average award of $12,500 is based on the three cases where damages amounts were specified. The pre-*Ward* average of $8,633 has been calculated by excluding the two exceptionally high amounts awarded by the courts in

generous award was one of $32,000 against Waterloo Regional Police Services by the Ontario Superior Court of Justice.[24] This award comprised special damages of $4,500, general damages of $25,000, and punitive damages of $2,500. *Charter* damages were awarded in this case without any specific reference to the *Ward* decision and without applying the four-stage liability *Ward* analysis.[25] The court did acknowledge that an award of punitive damages is to be given only in exceptional cases,[26] which may be an oblique acknowledgement of the discussion in *Ward*. However, the court explained, a message needed to be sent.[27] The court also acknowledged that the amount ($2,500) was nominal and not intended to overcompensate the claimant but rather to get the attention of the police.[28] One other award was for $5,000,[29] and another was for $500.[30] These awards might be looked upon as some evidence that lower courts in general will use the *Ward* compensation of $5,000 as a benchmark for wrongful detentions and strip searches.

D. ISSUES OF FAULT

One very noticeable effect of the *Ward*[31] decision upon post-*Ward Charter* cases is the very significant drop in the number of reported cases in which fault, or some type of mental state, was specifically required as a prerequisite to a successful *Charter* damages claim. In only four cases did the court specifically discuss the issue of fault as the basis for rejecting the *Charter* damages claim.[32] In three of these cases, the claimant or plaintiff had also made a claim in tort for malicious prosecution.[33] It is not too surprising, therefore, that a high standard of fault in the form of malice, *mala fides*, or improper motive became a factor in these *Charter* claims.

Patenaude v Roy (1994), 23 DLR (4th) 78 (Que CA) and *McTaggart v Ontario*, [2000] OTC 855 (SCJ). If the awards in these cases are included in the calculation, the average pre-*Ward* damages award increases significantly to $21,713. See Chapter 3, Section D.

24 See *Elliot*, above note 9.

25 See note 11, above.

26 *Elliot*, above note 9 at para 83.

27 *Ibid* at para 87.

28 *Ibid*.

29 See *Lamka*, above note 9.

30 See *Mason*, above note 9.

31 *Ward*, above note 1.

32 See note 16, above.

33 See *Forrest*, above note 14; *Elliot*, above note 9; *Henry* 2013 SC, above note 8.

In one of the three relevant cases, *Forrest v Ontario Provincial Police*,[34] the Ontario Divisional Court justified the application of the higher standard of malice by noting that McLachlin CJ in *Ward* had not specifically declared that *mala fides* was not required to prove a breach of the *Charter*.[35] The court in *Forrest* went on to point out that all the Chief Justice had required was proof of breach to satisfy step one of the new analytical approach.[36] Additional support for the position taken in favour of the higher standard by the Ontario court in *Forrest* might be found in the Chief Justice's suggestion that common law immunities are a source of "practical wisdom."[37]

There are, however, two post-*Ward* cases in which the courts, having to decide pre-trial issues involving the adequacy of the plaintiffs' pleadings, appeared to signal a less demanding fault standard.[38] In the first case, Robert Bilich sued the Toronto Police Services Board for $10 million.[39] He alleged that as a result of his arrest, his private civil rights and *Charter* rights had been violated. With regard to the *Charter* claim, Mr Bilich alleged violation of sections 7, 8, 9, 11(b), and 11(d). He based his section 11(b) claim upon an allegedly delayed and inadequate disclosure of information by the police that had caused the proceedings to be delayed. Justice Frank, of the Ontario Superior Court of Justice, struck down this claim, holding that it was the Crown, and the not the police, that was under a legal obligation to make full disclosure, and since the Crown had not been sued, the claim could not stand.[40] In respect of the *Charter* claims based on violations of sections 7, 8, 9, and 11(d), the defendant argued that they should also be struck because legal precedents required the plaintiff to allege and establish bad faith, *mala fides*, malice, or improper purposes as a prerequisite to the recovery of damages under the *Charter*. Justice Frank refused to do so, noting that the cases upon which the defendant relied pre-dated the *Ward* decision, which had declared that it was improper for a court to impose prescribed conditions on section 24(1). She therefore allowed the remaining *Charter* claims to stand.[41]

In the second case, *Henry v British Columbia (AG)*,[42] the claimant in his pleadings alleged that Crown prosecutors had wrongfully failed to disclose information to him, a failure that resulted in Mr Henry's being imprisoned.

---

34 *Forrest*, above note 14.
35 *Ibid* at para 51.
36 *Ibid*.
37 *Ward*, above note 1 at para 43.
38 See *Bilich*, above note 16; *Henry* 2013 SC, above note 8.
39 *Bilich*, above note 16.
40 *Ibid* at para 65.
41 *Ibid* at para 68. The reference by Frank J was to *Ward*, above note 1 at para 18.
42 *Henry* 2013 SC, above note 8.

This case is particularly significant for a number of reasons, besides the fact that it eventually made its way to the Supreme Court of Canada, where it was heard on 13 November 2014.[43] The *Henry* case is also important because the Supreme Court's decision in it changed the parameters of Crown liability in the area of wrongful failure to disclose information.

E. *HENRY v BRITISH COLUMBIA (AG)*: PROSECUTORIAL LIABILITY AND THE *WARD* CASE REVISITED

In terms of the evolution of *Charter* damages, the *Henry* case represents the first opportunity the Supreme Court has had to revisit its earlier decision in *Ward* and the new staged approach to *Charter* damages outlined in that case. For this reason, a close examination of *Henry*'s judicial history and of the judgments of the six Supreme Court justices who heard and decided the case is called for. What that panel had to say about *Ward*, its progeny, will hopefully prove instructive for lower courts in the future.

The *Henry* case began in 2011[44] when Mr Henry, representing himself, launched a civil suit against the City of Vancouver, the Attorney General of British Columbia, and the Attorney General of Canada, seeking damages for harm suffered as the result of a wrongful conviction that resulted in Mr Henry's being imprisoned for twenty-seven years. The suit would eventually make its way to the Supreme Court, with judgment rendered on 1 May 2015. The claim against the Attorney General of British Columbia alleged that the Crown had failed to make full disclosure of relevant information before, during, and after his trial. In his Notice of Civil Claim, Mr Henry pleaded various causes of action including negligence, malicious prosecution, misfeasance in public office, abuse of process, and breach of *Charter* sections 7 and 11(d).[45] The Attorney General of British Columbia moved to strike two of Mr Henry's causes of action, specifically those based on negligence and the *Charter*. In 2012, the negligence claim was struck by the application judge, Goepel J, because it was deemed to be inconsistent with *Nelles v Ontario*.[46] However, the judge did allow Mr Henry to proceed with his *Charter* claim because it was based on assertions of malicious prosecution. Justice Goepel cautioned Mr Henry that he would have to amend his proceedings if he intended to pursue his *Charter* damages claim against the

---

43 2015 SCC 24 [*Henry*].

44 See *Henry v British Columbia* (AG), 2012 BCSC 1401 [*Henry* 2012 SC], Goepel J, as referenced by Moldaver J in *Henry*, above note 43 at para 21.

45 See *Henry*, above note 43 at para 21.

46 [1989] 2 SCR 170 [*Nelles*]. See *Henry* 2012 SC, above note 44 at paras 43–60.

Attorney General of British Columbia, alleging conduct that fell short of malice.[47]

Mr Henry followed the court's suggestion and applied to amend his pleadings to allege that he was entitled to *Charter* damages against the province even though there was no finding that the acts of the prosecutors had been done maliciously.[48] The province opposed Mr Henry's application, but the City of Vancouver and Canada took no position on the proposed amendments. In those amendments, Mr Henry described the various acts and omissions of the Crown counsel as negligent, intentional, and malicious, and as being done in bad faith, contrary to the principles of fundamental justice, and with total disregard for the plaintiff's rights. As such, the acts, argued Mr Henry, were a marked and unacceptable departure from the reasonable standard to be expected of Crown counsel.[49] This standard, he noted, had its source in criminal actions, such as *R v 974649 Ontario Inc*,[50] that have relied on section 24(1) to support costs awards against the Crown for *Charter* breaches.[51] The province relied upon the Supreme Court decision in *Nelles*,[52] arguing that the long-standing rule of prosecutorial immunity reflected in that case required malicious conduct on the part of the prosecutor to be alleged and proven.[53]

After considering the arguments of both parties, Goepel J declared, "I see no need to limit an individual's claim for *Charter* damages by importing the malice requirement which governs private law actions for malicious prosecution. In my view the good governance concerns can be properly protected by applying the standard that has been followed in the criminal costs cases."[54] The application judge therefore concluded that a claim lies against the province for *Charter* damages if the plaintiff can establish that Crown counsel acted in a marked and unacceptable departure from the reasonable standard expected of Crown counsel.[55] In his view, such a pleading disclosed a cause of action known to the law, and he therefore granted the amendment.[56]

---

47 See *Henry* 2012 SC, above note 44 at paras 61–72.
48 *Henry* 2013 SC, above note 8.
49 *Ibid* at para 9.
50 2001 SCC 81 [*974649 Ontario*].
51 *Henry* 2013 SC, above note 8 at para 14.
52 *Nelles*, above note 46.
53 *Henry* 2013 SC, above note 8 at paras 10 and 12.
54 *Ibid* at para 61.
55 *Ibid* at para 62.
56 *Ibid* at para 64.

The Crown appealed Goepel J's decision to the British Columbia Court of Appeal.[57] Justice Hall speaking for a unanimous court held that the chambers judge ought to have refused the amendment to the pleading because the language of the amendment appeared to sanction a standard of liability or fault that he described as "a form of negligence akin to that species often referred to as 'gross negligence,' a type of conduct that allowed recovery in earlier times in motor vehicle cases involving gratuitous passengers . . . ."[58] It was Hall J's view that this would create a new head of liability against prosecutors that would conflict with existing Supreme Court jurisprudence, and that such an expansion of liability should be undertaken only by a legislature or the Supreme Court.[59]

A more detailed examination and comparison of the decisions of Goepel J and the Court of Appeal may help the interested observer understand why they reached different conclusions, apart from the natural and traditionally more conservative or cautious approach usually adopted by appeal courts to new departures from existing legal principles.

The application judge justified his decision to allow a lower standard of fault to be pleaded on several grounds. First, section 24(1) damages had been used in criminal cases to award costs on the basis of what the Court of Appeal would describe as a form of gross negligence.[60] Second, in his opinion, the *Nelles* decision could not be read as deciding that *Charter* actions against prosecutors could only be brought in circumstances where malice, as defined in that case, was established.[61] A review of post-*Nelles* Canadian authorities led him to conclude that they did not support the *Nelles* requirement of malice.[62] He declared that at most the Court in *Nelles* had left the question open.[63] Justice Goepel made no reference to other Supreme Court cases, such as *Proulx v Quebec (AG)*[64] and *Miazga v Kvello Estate*,[65] that the Court of Appeal would declare had set the parameters of civil liability for prosecutorial misconduct and were binding on lower courts.[66] Third, Goepel J agreed with the comments of Frank J in *Bilich v Toronto (City) Police Services*

57 *Henry* CA, above note 8.
58 *Ibid* at para 20.
59 *Ibid* at paras 20 and 29.
60 *Henry* 2013 SC, above note 8 at para 14.
61 *Ibid* at para 45.
62 *Ibid* at para 56.
63 *Ibid* at para 57.
64 2001 SCC 66.
65 2009 SCC 51.
66 *Henry* CA, above note 8 at paras 28 & 29.

Board[67] that decisions requiring bad faith, malice, or improper purposes as a prerequisite to a claim for *Charter* damages needed to be reconsidered in light of the instructions in *Ward*[68] that "it is improper for courts to reduce their discretion to award Charter damages 'by casting it in a strait-jacket of judicially prescribed conditions.'"[69] Justice Goepel also invoked the Supreme Court decisions in *974649 Ontario* and *Doucet-Boudreau v Nova Scotia (Minister of Education)*[70] to support a judicial approach that would give section 24(1) a broad and purposive interpretation. Finally, it was his view that good governance concerns could be properly protected by applying the standard that had been used in criminal costs cases.[71]

By contrast, Hall J for the British Columbia Court of Appeal took the position that costs cases were not a suitable paradigm for non-disclosure situations because the costs remedy had been created by courts to help them control their own processes and provide a speedy remedy for prosecutorial lapses occurring during trial. As such, the remedy was quite different from the constitutional remedy of *Charter* damages.[72] As already noted, the Court of Appeal declared that there was "a consistent line of authority from the Supreme Court of Canada" that applied.[73] This line of authority, Hall J stated, had not been altered by *Ward* because *Ward* was not a case about prosecutorial discretion.[74] By implication, the Court of Appeal appears to be saying that the instructions from the *Ward* decision quoted by Goepel J regarding a judicial strait-jacket do not apply. In any event, Hall J also noted that the Supreme Court in *Ward* had pointed out that good governance concerns could operate to militate against an award of *Charter* damages.[75] The Court of Appeal did not directly address the issue of good governance concerns, but its expressed fear that the sanctioned amendment would lower prosecutorial protection from liability and create a new threshold of fault seems to clearly reflect by implication a concern that the new standard would not provide adequate protection and would therefore be a good governance concern.

On a final note of comparison, while Goepel J had been prepared to change the existing law with regard to the parameters of prosecutorial

---

67 *Bilich*, above note 16.

68 *Ward*, above note 1.

69 *Henry* 2013 SC, above note 8 at para 57.

70 2003 SCC 62.

71 *Henry* 2013 SC, above note 8 at para 61.

72 *Henry* CA, above note 8 at para 27.

73 *Ibid* at para 28.

74 *Ibid*.

75 *Ibid*.

liability, the Court of Appeal thought this was a bridge too far, one that should be built and crossed only by the legislature or the Supreme Court. An interested observer may be led to speculate why Goepel J took the risk that he did by allowing Mr Henry to plead a lower standard of fault. Mr Henry had certainly suffered grievous consequences as a result of the alleged failure of the Crown to fully disclose relevant and material information to him, and the need for a *Charter* remedy if his allegations were proven seemed very strong. This factor and the strong Supreme Court encouragement to lower-court judges to give section 24(1) a generous and purposive interpretation were apparently sufficient to convince Goepel J to take the risk that he did. A closer look at the facts of the *Henry* case may provide a better understanding of the difficult task that all three courts, including the Supreme Court, had to face in trying to reach a balanced decision in this case.[76]

In 1983, Mr Henry was convicted by a jury of ten sexual offences, declared a dangerous offender, and sentenced to an indefinite period of incarceration. He was imprisoned for twenty-seven years. It was his contention that he had been wrongfully convicted because the Crown had failed to make full disclosure of relevant information before, during, and after his trial. Specifically, he claimed that he had asked for statements from all his alleged victims as well as medical and forensic files but that, in spite of his request, the Crown had not disclosed any of the requested information before the trial began. At the commencement of the trial, Mr Henry, representing himself, had once more requested disclosure of all victims' statements. In response, the Crown had supplied him with eleven statements made by eight trial complainants but withheld approximately thirty additional statements made by other complainants. These latter statements would have revealed inconsistencies that could have been used to attack already suspect identification evidence put forward by the Crown. The Crown had also withheld forensic evidence that might have implicated another suspect.

Between 1984 and 2006, Mr Henry filed more than fifty applications in different courts and with the federal Crown seeking to have his convictions reviewed while continuing to seek disclosure relating to his own case. Eventually, in 2010, as a result of new evidence that was discovered as part of an investigation into a number of unsolved sexual attacks that had occurred between 1983 and 1988, the British Columbia Court of Appeal considered his case on the merits and found a number of errors serious enough to prevent

76 For Moldaver J's detailed outline of the factual history of the *Henry* case, see *Henry*, above note 43 at paras 4–21.

proof of identification.[77] A unanimous Court of Appeal held that the previous verdicts had been unwarranted and ordered Mr Henry acquitted on all ten convictions. It was against this background that Mr Henry commenced his civil action in 2011, which ultimately led him to the Supreme Court in 2014.[78]

After being rebuffed by the British Columbia Court of Appeal in early 2014,[79] Mr Henry made application to the Supreme Court for leave to appeal his case. The application was filed in February 2014, submitted to the Court in April 2014, and granted on 15 May 2014. A motion to state a constitutional question or questions was granted on 9 June 2014.[80] The constitutional question was posed in the following way: "Does s. 24(1) of the *Canadian Charter of Rights and Freedoms* authorize a court of competent jurisdiction to award damages against the Crown for prosecutorial misconduct absent proof of malice?"[81]

Because the issue of prosecutorial liability was so important, the case attracted the attention of many in the legal community. Besides Mr Henry and the Attorney General of British Columbia, there were a number of intervenors before the Supreme Court, who either submitted written briefs or presented oral submissions. The Attorney General of Canada and all the provincial attorneys general except that of Prince Edward Island were represented, as well as the Canadian Association of Crown Counsel and a number of other associations.[82] The seven-person panel hearing the case consisted of McLachlin CJ and Moldaver, Abella, Wagner, Gascon, LeBel, and Karakatsanis JJ. Justice LeBel took no part in the judgment, so the decision rendered was the product of six Supreme Court justices, two of whom had taken part in the *Ward*[83] decision: McLachlin CJ and Abella J.

All six Supreme Court justices answered the constitutional question in the affirmative. Four of the justices — Moldaver, Abella, Wagner, and Gascon JJ — limited the question to the narrower issue of prosecutorial wrongdoing in the context of a wrongful failure to disclose relevant and material evidence to the claimant (defendant).[84] And they went the further

---

77 *R v Henry*, 2010 BCCA 462 at para 154.
78 *Henry*, above note 43.
79 *Henry* CA, above note 8.
80 *Henry v British Columbia* (*AG*), [2014] SCCA No 70 [*Henry* SCC Motion].
81 *Henry*, above note 43 at para 30.
82 *Henry* SCC Motion, above note 80 at para 3.
83 *Ward*, above note 1.
84 *Henry*, above note 43 at paras 32 & 33.

step of outlining what the claimant had to establish in lieu of malice. As they explained,

> a cause of action will lie where the Crown, in breach of its constitutional obligations, causes harm to the accused by intentionally withholding information when it knows, or would reasonably be expected to know, that the information is material to the defence and that the failure to disclose will likely impinge on the accused's ability to make full answer and defence.[85]

In the view of the majority, this standard represented a high threshold for a successful *Charter* damages claim even though it was a lower threshold than malice.[86]

The remaining two justices — McLachlin CJ and Karakatsanis J — dealt with Mr Henry's case as a disclosure issue without specifically stating that they agreed with the majority's limitation of the constitutional question. They disagreed more fundamentally with the majority's decision to require any fault standard, be it malice or the one proposed by Moldaver J and his concurring justices. As McLachlin CJ explained, "[i]mposing a fault requirement for *Charter* damages, where the Crown has breached its duty to disclose, is inconsistent with the purpose of s. 24(1) and with the principled framework established in *Vancouver (City) v. Ward* . . . for assessing whether an award of damages would be appropriate and just in the circumstances of a particular case."[87] In her view, there was "no principled basis for imposing any threshold of fault or intention on Mr. Henry's claim . . . ."[88] As a result, McLachlin CJ and Karakatsanis J, like the Moldaver J majority, were prepared to allow the appeal and grant the application to amend. However, they made it clear that all Mr Henry had to allege in his pleadings was that "the Crown breached its constitutional obligation to disclose relevant information and that *Charter* damages would be an appropriate and just remedy, serving one or more of the functions of compensation, vindication and deterrence."[89] Mr Henry did not have to allege that "the Crown breached its constitutional obligation intentionally, or with malice, in order to access *Charter* damages."[90] To more fully understand why the Supreme Court was divided on what Mr Henry's amended pleadings should allege, it is necessary

85 *Ibid* at para 31.
86 *Ibid.*
87 *Ibid* at para 104.
88 *Ibid* at para 133.
89 *Ibid* at para 138.
90 *Ibid.*

to examine more closely the approaches taken by the two groups of justices to other more specific issues in the case.

1) Modification of the *Ward* Four-Step Liability Approach

The different approaches taken by the two groups to the issue of what would be an acceptable threshold of fault in lieu of malice reveal a number of subissues on which the two groups both agreed and disagreed, all in the context of failure to disclose. The most significant point of disagreement related to Moldaver J's apparent modification of the *Ward* staged approach to a *Charter* claim for damages. By requiring a claimant to establish intention and knowledge at the proof of breach stage (step one), the majority appear to have specifically inserted a fault element at the beginning of the claim process rather than letting it emerge later in step three as part of the discussion of countervailing factors such as good governance. As outlined in *Ward*,[91] step one makes no specific reference to fault as an element that the claimant must establish as part of the proof of a *Charter* violation. In *Henry*, McLachlin CJ makes it clear that at step one of the *Ward* approach, a claimant need prove only a factual breach, and need not prove fault at all.[92] To use her words, "There is . . . no principled basis for imposing any threshold of fault or intention on Mr. Henry's claim for *Charter* damages . . . ."[93] Justice Moldaver tried to offset this objection by suggesting that the new test did not require the claimant to prove any mental element such as intention because both intention and knowledge could be inferred and imputed.[94]

2) Countervailing Factors

Countervailing factors are another issue on which Moldaver J and McLachlin CJ appear to have differed. Justice Moldaver mentioned the availability of alternative remedies but made no reference to whether Mr Henry had or did not have any in this case.[95] Instead, Moldaver J seems to have thought that only good governance concerns were at issue in this case.[96] By contrast, McLachlin CJ appears to have been concerned that there might not be an alternative remedy for Mr Henry that would fulfill the functional objectives

91 *Ward*, above note 1.
92 *Henry*, above note 43 at paras 109 and 138.
93 *Ibid* at para 133.
94 *Ibid* at paras 86 and 88.
95 *Ibid* at para 38.
96 *Ibid* at para 39. Justice Moldaver discusses "good governance" concerns *ibid* at paras 39–43.

of *Charter* damages.[97] As to the good governance concerns raised by the Attorney General of British Columbia, McLachlin CJ found them to be misplaced.[98] The whole issue of prosecutorial discretion, in her view, was not relevant because wrongful failure to disclose did not involve the exercise of prosecutorial discretion in the usual sense of the term as it had been discussed in *Nelles*.[99]

3) Discretion

Justice Moldaver and McLachlin CJ agreed that Crown prosecutors have a constitutional obligation to disclose material evidence to defendants.[100] However, they disagreed about the effect of this constitutional obligation on prosecutorial discretion, with McLachlin CJ maintaining that there existed an absolute legal obligation with regard to disclosure matters, leaving no room for the exercise of discretion whatever.[101] Justice Moldaver does not appear to have been prepared to go that far, stating that there were still situations involving disclosure where Crown prosecutors had to make what he called "judgment calls."[102]

In the broader context of government actors exercising discretion in the process of carrying out their governmental functions, McLachlin CJ conceded that *Ward* had recognized that there might be a need for limited immunity from section 24(1) damages claims for a *Charter* breach that arose from the exercise of a general discretion.[103] As she explained, the Crown would raise the need for this immunity protection at step three of the *Ward* framework, thus placing the onus on the claimant to prove malice or some other standard of fault.[104] All this would be part of the government's attempt to convince the court that good governance concerns militated against *Charter* damages being awarded.

---

97 *Ibid* at para 122.
98 *Ibid* at paras 120 and 127.
99 *Nelles*, above note 46.
100 *Henry*, above note 43 at para 59, Moldaver J, and paras 128 and 138, McLachlin CJ.
101 *Ibid* at paras 128 and 138.
102 *Ibid* at para 60.
103 *Ibid* at para 126.
104 *Ibid* at para 119.

4) Causation

Although not the subject of prior discussion in the *Henry* case, Moldaver J, looking ahead to the prospect of a trial, discussed the issue of causation and the need for the claimant to prove that any damages or injuries suffered were the result of a *Charter* breach by Crown counsel.[105] In this regard, he referenced the "but for" test of causation.[106] His discussion of *Charter* damages focused on the compensation purpose of such damages and made no mention of vindication or deterrence as the other purposes of *Charter* damages. His argument seems to suggest that *Charter* damages will be available only if the complainant can prove a causal connection between actual harm or damage and the *Charter* breach by the defendant. Chief Justice McLachlin appears to have had difficulty with this approach, pointing out that ". . . *Ward* holds explicitly that damages may be appropriate and just even where no causal connection is established between a *Charter* breach and harm suffered by the claimant . . . ."[107] She also pointed out that *Ward*[108] had proposed that in cases where the objectives of vindication and deterrence called for an award, the fact that the claimant had not suffered any personal loss would not preclude *Charter* damages being awarded.[109] She concluded that the "but for" test may not be appropriate in the *Henry* case, but since the issue had been neither addressed in the decisions below nor argued before the Supreme Court, she was prepared to leave further discussion for another day.[110]

5) The Private Law Standard of Malice

Justice Moldaver concluded that *Nelles*[111] and its progeny were not dispositive of the *Henry* case for two reasons.[112] First, the private law tort of malicious prosecution is an eighteenth-century remedy developed to control potential abuses by private citizens commencing and continuing private prosecutions.[113] By implication, such a remedy is no longer suitable for mod-

---

105 *Ibid* at paras 95–98.
106 As he explained, *ibid* at para 95, "[l]iability attaches to the Crown only upon a finding of 'but for' causation."
107 *Ibid* at para 117.
108 *Ward*, above note 1.
109 *Henry*, above note 43 at para 117.
110 *Ibid* at para 118.
111 *Nelles*, above note 46.
112 *Henry*, above note 43 at para 56.
113 *Ibid* at para 57.

ern situations involving wrongful non-disclosure of evidence by a public Crown prosecutor in a *Charter* case. Second, the purposive approach to section 24(1) militates against proof of malice.[114] Justice Moldaver did, however, concede that "the policy factors outlined in *Nelles* inform the liability threshold in this case."[115]

Chief Justice McLachlin did not directly address the issue of private law as a guide beyond noting that "[w]here breaches of the duty to disclose occur, *Charter* liability flows from the constitutionally entrenched mechanisms that permit individuals to hold the state to account. This is distinct from tort liability, which imposes conduct-based thresholds to regulate tortious conduct as between individuals."[116] It would seem that for the Chief Justice, in the area of non-disclosure, private law is not needed to inform the court about thresholds because the constitutional obligation to disclose makes this unnecessary.

6) International Obligations

The Chief Justice argued that "[t]o require proof of intention would be to lower *Charter* protection below the level of protection found in an international human rights instrument that Canada has ratified."[117] It was her view that Canada's commitment to provide compensation to those who have been wrongfully convicted, as expressed in article 14(6) of the *International Covenant on Civil and Political Rights*,[118] supported the conclusion that Mr Henry need not establish fault to justify an award of damages under section 24(1). Justice Moldaver made no reference to international obligations at all.

7) *Henry*: Concluding Observations

The Supreme Court in *Henry* established that the traditional private law standard of malice, as exemplified by the tort of malicious prosecution, did not apply in cases where Crown counsel wrongfully failed to make full disclosure of relevant information to the defendant in a criminal case. By so doing, the Court changed the law in this specific area. The Supreme Court also stated that the new test created by the change in the law would apply at

114 *Ibid* at para 64.

115 *Ibid* at para 66.

116 *Ibid* at para 129.

117 *Ibid* at para 137.

118 16 December 1966, 999 UNTS 171 (entered into force 23 March 1976, accession by Canada 19 May 1976).

both the pleading stage and the trial stage of cases where the claimant was asking for *Charter* damages as a remedy. As the Court explained, to withstand a motion to strike at the pleading stage in civil litigation, a claimant need only plead facts that, taken to be true, would be sufficient to support a finding on each element of the test.[119] At trial, a claimant would have to convince the finder of fact that the same elements of the new test were also established.

By making this change, the Supreme Court appears to have modified the staged approach that it formulated in *Ward*.[120] According to this approach, the claimant at stage one need only establish factual breach of *Charter* provisions without more. No evidence or allegations of fault or of the defendant's mental state need be presented. As a result of the *Henry* decision, lower courts will have to ask themselves whether the modified approach and test applies more generally to other *Charter* damages claims and in other areas of state activity. If the policy concern that appears to have influenced Moldaver J and his concurring justices, namely, the need for some kind of legal filter to exclude marginal claims against Crown prosecutors at an early stage of the litigation process, is valid, then it may be equally applicable in other areas of state activity as well.

A collateral effect of the new approach and test might be to give fault or other mental elements, such as intention, a more prominent role in the judicial analysis of *Charter* damages claims. This might happen despite Moldaver J's attempt to mollify such concerns by declaring that the elements of intent and knowledge are not designed to place "an undue burden on claimants to prove subjective mental states" but to address good governance concerns by setting "a sufficiently high threshold . . . ."[121] There is no question, however, that since the Court has made intention a significant element of the step one inquiry as to whether the *Charter* has been breached, instead of merely one factor to be considered later on in the step three analysis of countervailing factors such as good governance concerns, fault or intention might become a critical factor in the analysis of *Charter* damages claims by lower courts in the future. If the foregoing analysis is accurate, then perhaps we are witness to the initial development of a third countervailing consideration, that being the protection of the judicial system from a flood of marginal claims for *Charter* damages.

The *Henry* decision, in addition to fuelling the foregoing speculation about its potentially broad implications for *Charter* damages claims gener-

---

119 *Henry*, above note 43 at para 85.

120 *Ward*, above note 1.

121 *Henry*, above note 43 at para 89.

ally, also provides glimpses of the current Supreme Court's view of damages as a new constitutional remedy. Given the different makeup of the Court in *Henry*, the justices' views of the *Ward* approach should be relevant and informative. Justice Moldaver, speaking for his other three concurring justices, made several interesting and significant observations about *Charter* damages as remedy. He noted that they were still evolving and must be allowed to develop, albeit slowly rather than rapidly, that courts needed to be careful not to stifle that development, and that, on the other hand, courts must be careful not to extend the remedy too far.[122] Justice Moldaver also cautioned that courts should not try to make damages one remedy for all *Charter* wrongs. In his words, ". . . *Charter* damages are not a silver bullet. They are just one of many remedies that may be available to individuals whose *Charter* rights have been breached . . . ."[123] Overall, Moldaver J's approach to *Charter* damages and their development could be described as cautiously optimistic.

Chief Justice McLachlin, on the other hand, focused her comments primarily on the need to provide effective remedies for *Charter* breaches, emphasizing that section 24 should be given a generous and purposive interpretation and that the discretion provided by that section should not be reduced by some kind of binding formula that would apply to all cases.[124] The Chief Justice clearly thought that the Moldaver approach, with a single standard involving intention applied to step one as a prerequisite to a claim's going any further, was an example of such a formula. She acknowledged that the courts' discretion was not unfettered, but she preferred a case-by-case evaluation of what the court considered to be an appropriate and just remedy at step three of the *Ward* analysis, when countervailing considerations could be discussed and evaluated.[125] Lower courts examining her words might easily conclude that in other *Charter* damages claims, that is, those not involving prosecutorial full-disclosure issues, the Moldaver approach should not be used. The extent to which lower courts should in the future impose constraints on the judicial discretion provided by section 24, apart from the guidance given by the Supreme Court in *Ward*, was not discussed by the Chief Justice, nor was any guidance given.

Given Mr Henry's particular situation, his *Charter* damages claim cannot be described as frivolous or vexatious. Justice Moldaver seemed to think

---

122 *Ibid* at paras 35 and 41: Justice Moldaver suggested that the establishment of a high threshold should circumscribe the availability of *Charter* damages.

123 *Ibid* at para 36.

124 *Ibid* at para 105.

125 *Ibid* at paras 120 and 126.

that Mr Henry could, at trial, meet the high standard proposed by the Supreme Court.[126] Chief Justice McLachlin did not directly address the question, but she did have some concerns. She pointed out that it was far from clear that Mr Henry had any alternative remedy that would "fulfill the functional objectives of *Charter* damages."[127] In her opinion, if this proved to be the case and if no remedy was available under section 24(1) because of the new high standard being imposed, Mr Henry might be left without a remedy at all.[128] Given the facts of Mr Henry's situation, her concerns may not be entirely warranted. If Mr Henry can prove his allegations at trial, it seems very likely that the egregious behaviour of Crown counsel in this case will meet the newly minted standard. It is possible, of course, that the Chief Justice was more concerned with the *Ward* approach's modification, by which fault would be specifically addressed at step one rather than step three.

Although courts will continue to have the difficult task of finding for different situations the right balance between a qualification for the *Charter* damages test that is not too high and one that is not too low, the *Henry* case does not seem to be the best example to demonstrate the need for a legal filter at step one of the *Charter* damages claim.

F. USE OF THE *WARD* TEST IN NON-*CHARTER* CASES

It is very interesting to note that the *Ward*[129] decision has been discussed and applied by lower courts and tribunals in eight non-*Charter* cases involving family, labour, human rights, and privacy law issues.[130] In cases involving compensation claims for statutory violations, adjudicating bodies have turned to the *Ward* decision for general guidance on the damages issue. The

126 *Ibid* at para 81.

127 *Ibid* at para 122.

128 *Ibid* at para 134.

129 *Ward*, above note 1.

130 The eight non-*Charter* cases comprise three human rights cases, two cases involving the federal *Privacy Act*, and one case each involving the *Official Languages Act*, family law issues, and labour law issues. For a list of these cases, see Appendix 21. In *Lavigne v Canada (Office of the Commissioner of Official Languages)*, [2002] 2 SCR 773 at para 25, Gonthier J referred to the *Official Languages Act* and the *Privacy Act* as having quasi-constitutional status: "The *Official Languages Act* and the *Privacy Act* are closely linked to the values and rights set out in the Constitution, and this explains the quasi-constitutional status that this Court has recognized them as having." Discussion then took place on the proper approach to the interpretation of these statutes and did not involve *Charter* issues or *Charter* damages.

Ontario Human Rights Tribunal has been particularly interested in the Supreme Court of Canada's views on compensation for injury to intangible interests such as emotional distress in the form of loss of dignity, humiliation, embarrassment, or hurt feelings. These types of emotional reactions to an unlawful act would not normally be compensated according to private law damages principles, but the Supreme Court made it clear in *Ward* that they were compensable when the result of violations of public law provisions like the *Charter*. With the *Ward* analysis to support its decisions, the Ontario tribunal made awards of $4,000,[131] $25,000,[132] and $10,000.[133]

G. GENERAL CONCLUSIONS

It is still too early to accurately assess the full impact of the *Ward*[134] decision upon the evolution of *Charter* damages. Clearly, lower courts have benefitted from the analysis provided by the Supreme Court of Canada in *Ward* as to the meaning of "appropriate" and "just" and as to the functional role that damages should play as a *Charter* remedy. Lower courts now have the benefit of the Supreme Court's decision in *Henry*,[135] which appears to expand the remedial scope of section 24(1) at least in the rather narrow confines of the Crown's failure to disclose. But the legal profession and some lower courts may take this case as a signal that step one of the *Ward* approach should be modified. Speculation aside, with the limited post-*Ward* data available, it is still too early to attempt a definitive assessment of *Ward*'s impact on *Charter* damages claims and to offer reliable conclusions.

131 *Arunachalam v Best Buy Canada*, 2010 HRTO 1880, referring, *ibid* at para 46, to *Ward*, above note 1 at para 27.

132 *De Abreo v Humber Institute of Technology & Advanced Learning*, 2010 HRTO 2404, referring, *ibid* at para 85, to *Ward*, above note 1 at para 27.

133 *Palangio v The Corporation of the Town of Cochrane*, 2011 HRTO 1491, referring, *ibid* at para 55, to *Ward*, above note 1 at para 27.

134 *Ward*, above note 1.

135 *Henry*, above note 43.

Chapter 8

Final Observations and Conclusions

A. EFFECTIVENESS OF DAMAGES AS A *CHARTER* REMEDY

The Supreme Court of Canada in *Vancouver (City) v Ward*[1] did not attempt an evaluation of the effectiveness of damages as a *Canadian Charter of Rights and Freedoms*[2] remedy. This is not surprising since such an evaluation was not required to dispose of the legal issues before the Court. In any event, trying to measure with any degree of accuracy the practical effectiveness of a *Charter* remedy presents a real challenge. One approach would be to try to assess the perceived deterrent effect of damages remedies and the degree of satisfaction or remedial value experienced by individual claimants who have received damages awards for violations of their *Charter* rights. Unfortunately, obtaining reliable objective data relevant to these factors would be either too expensive or impossible. It is impossible to determine the number of potential *Charter* violators who may have been deterred because of the availability of a remedy like *Charter* damages. Successful claimants who have received an award could be polled to establish their degree or level of satisfaction, but such an exercise would be expensive. We can assume that the satisfaction rate of unsuccessful claimants would be low.

What is possible is to measure the effectiveness of *Charter* damages in terms of (1) frequency of use, (2) the success rate, and (3) the amount of damages awarded. Fortunately, these types of data have been captured by

1 2010 SCC 27, var'g (*sub nom Ward v Vancouver (City)*) 2009 BCCA 23, var'g 2007 BCSC 3 [*Ward*].

2 Part I of the *Constitution Act, 1982*, being Schedule B to the *Canada Act 1982* (UK), 1982, c 11 [*Charter*].

the survey in this book and provide a useful starting point from which to attempt an assessment. A review of five different *Charter* remedies claimed or provided by courts under the authority of section 24(1) of the *Charter* during the period 1984 to 2007 produces useful and interesting data.[3] The five remedies selected for study were (1) stay of proceedings, (2) miscellaneous judicial orders, (3) declaration of *Charter* breach, (4) legal costs, and (5) damages. Statistical data reveals that damages remedies were the least frequently claimed or awarded, accounting for only 7.5 percent of the total number of remedies involved. By contrast, the most favoured remedy was a stay of proceedings, with a frequency of use rate of 63 percent, a rate more than five times greater than the second most common remedy, miscellaneous judicial orders, with a use rate of 12 percent. Declarations of *Charter* breach ranked third with a use rate of 10 percent while legal costs ranked fourth with a use rate of 8 percent, slightly ahead of damages in last place.[4]

The most sought-after section 24 remedy was exclusion of evidence under section 24(2).[5] There was exactly the same number of remedies claimed or provided under this section as there was number of all five remedies claimed or provided under section 24(1) combined (917). This is because the majority of claims for *Charter* remedies arose in the context of criminal proceedings, which also accounts for the stay of proceedings being the most favoured remedy under section 24(1).

If, besides the frequency of use rate, one was to take into account the success rate of *Charter* damages claims as an indicator of effectiveness, the success rate of 35 percent for the period 1984 to 2010 (not 1984 to 2007) could be considered significant but not outstanding.[6] However, this rate was achieved in the face of the Crown's ability to raise the defence of qualified immunity, a defence that increases the claimant's burden of proving a *Charter* violation. Achieving a success rate of 35 percent in this context makes it more significant. A less encouraging factor is the size of the average pre-*Ward Charter* damages award. An award of $8,633 could be described as modest.[7] Such an award is not likely to provide a claimant's lawyer with

---

3 The period 1984 to 2007 was selected because of the coverage of *Charter* cases and remedies granted by the courts in the *Charter of Rights Decisions* reporter for these years (Vancouver: Western Legal Publications, 1982) (loose-leaf).

4 See Appendix 22.

5 See *ibid*.

6 See Chapter 7, Section B.

7 This average award amount excludes two exceptionally high awards of $100,000 and $230,000 in *Patenaude v Roy* (1994), 23 DLR (4th) 78 (Que CA), and *McTaggart v Ontario*, [2000] OTC 855 (SCJ), respectively. If these

much incentive to pursue a *Charter* claim in light of the high costs of litigation.

An analysis of the *Charter* damages awards from 1984 to 2010 shows that 60 percent of the awards were for an amount below $10,000.[8] As far as deterrence is concerned, being ordered to pay a total of $80,000 in *Charter* damages, as the defendant was ordered to do by the British Columbia Court of Appeal in *Auton (Guardian ad litem of) v British Columbia (Minister of Health)*,[9] even though the award was later overturned by the Supreme Court, could reasonably be viewed by the defendant as a significant deterrent. Looking at the survey data, however, one can see that punitive damages specifically were awarded in only six cases, or 24 percent of the total number of successful cases.[10] In two of these cases, the punitive award was substantial ($50,000 and $20,000), but the average award in the remaining four cases was only $938. Given the difficulties and uncertainties involved in determining what is an appropriate and just award for the purposes of vindication of rights and deterrence of wrongful state behaviour, as well as the recognized reluctance of other countries' courts to award punitive damages specifically as part of public law damages,[11] an increase in post-*Ward Charter* damages to fulfill the purposes of vindication and deterrence does not seem likely.

For the purposes of this book's survey, cases involving criminal proceedings in which either the claimant requested legal costs or the court awarded them have not been included. Legal costs were not considered to be a true damages remedy because in almost all cases where they were awarded it was not to compensate for a violation of *Charter* rights but, rather, to enforce disclosure requirements in criminal proceedings. Were damages and legal costs to be considered complementary remedies because of their common compensation element, their combined frequency of use rate in relation to other *Charter* remedies would be 15 percent, second only to the stay remedy.[12] However, even this combined damages remedy would remain a distant second and still represent a low percentage of use.

Post-*Ward* decisions covering the period 2010 to 2014 show a marked increase in the number of *Charter* damages claims filed and disposed of by

---

two awards are included, the average *Charter* damages amount increases to $21,713. See Chapter 3, Section D.

8 See Appendix 5.

9 2002 BCCA 538, var'g 2001 BCSC 220, rev'd 2004 SCC 78.

10 See Appendix 10 and *McTaggart v Ontario*, [2000] OTC 855 (SCJ).

11 See *Ward*, above note 1 at para 56.

12 See Appendix 22.

the courts per year. Cases heard by the courts increased from 2.6 cases per year for the period 1984 to 2010 to 7.3 cases per year for the period 2010 to the end of 2014.[13] While the success rate for this period was much lower, the average damages award increased from $8,633 to $12,500.[14] Admittedly, the amount of data is quite limited. A longer post-*Ward* period could perhaps produce different and more reliable results.

B. WHY THE MODEST USE OF THE DAMAGES REMEDY?

The findings noted above are most likely the result of a number of different factors. In 1995, after a decade of judicial experience with the *Charter* and section 24(1), one legal academic issued a cautionary note about the potential effectiveness of damages as a *Charter* remedy. Professor Mullen suggested a number of reasons why, up until 1995, damages had not been a commonly sought or awarded remedy. Among other reasons, he pointed to the following:[15]

1) the limited or restrictive definition that courts had given to the concept of government or governmental activities
2) a similar limiting interpretation that courts had applied to the scope or reach of *Charter* sections 7 and 15
3) application of the rule in *Schachter v Canada*,[16] which prevents concurrent remedies being awarded pursuant to sections 52 and 24(1) in almost all situations
4) the judicial imposition of a high degree or standard of fault, a by-product of the courts' acceptance of the qualified immunity defence
5) the limited jurisdiction of provincial criminal courts to award civil damages
6) the reluctance of courts to recognize *per se* violations of the *Charter*

To these factors may be added the exclusion of *Charter* damages claims due to an overlap or conflict with tort actions.[17] Professor Mullan did not cite a

---

13 Representing thirty-three cases in four and a half years.

14 The average award for the three successful cases was $12,500.

15 David J Mullan, "Damages for Violation of Constitutional Rights — A False Spring?" (1995) 6 *National Journal of Constitutional Law* 103.

16 [1992] 2 SCR 679.

17 This appears to be a diminishing reason for rejection of *Charter* damages claims, with only five of the seventy-one pre-*Ward* cases being affected: *Breen v Saunders* (1986), 71 NBR (2d) 404 (QB); *Charters v Harper* (1987), 79 NBR (2d) 28 (QB); *Bauder v Wilson* (1988), 43 CRR 149 (BCSC); *Jane Doe v Toronto*

lack of governing principles, or a clear analytical framework to guide lower courts in their *Charter* damages decisions, as a negative influence, but he did note the lack of such principles.[18]

Nineteen years later, most of the negative factors discussed by Professor Mullan, with one possible exception, are still having an impact on *Charter* damages claims. The one exception appears to be a clear increase in the number of section 15 cases reported.[19] A second significant development is the analytical framework provided by the Supreme Court of Canada in *Ward*.[20] Understandably, the impact of each of Mullan's factors is probably different. The study presented here suggests that two negative factors are particularly significant in their effect upon the use and availability of *Charter* damages.

The first is one referenced by Professor Mullan: the limited jurisdiction of provincial criminal courts to award *Charter* damages in criminal cases.[21] Mullan points out that a provincial criminal court is limited to issuing an acquittal, a stay of proceedings, a refusal to admit evidence (under section 24(2)), or an order for costs.[22] The survey data presented here on the use of remedies pursuant to section 24(1) supports the view that the limited jurisdiction of provincial criminal courts negatively impacts the use of *Charter* damages. If a victim of a *Charter* violation occurring in the course of a provincial criminal court proceeding wants to pursue a claim for *Charter* damages, she will have to initiate a separate civil action with all the additional costs associated with that action. The *Ward* decision in 2010 did address this issue specifically. Chief Justice McLachlin, speaking for the Court, declared, "Generally, the appropriate forum for an award of damages under s. 24(1) is a court which has the power to consider *Charter* questions and which by statute or inherent jurisdiction has the power to award damages. Provincial criminal courts are not so empowered and thus do not have the power to award damages under s. 24(1)."[23] The jurisdictional limitation that concerned Professor Mullan in 1995 remains unchanged.

The second important negative factor made evident by the survey data is the judicial application of the very high standard of malice to *Charter*

(Metropolitan) Commissioners of Police (1998), 39 OR (3d) 487 (Gen Div); *Ernst v Quinonez*, [2003] OTC 847 (SCJ).

18 Mullan, above note 15 at 106.

19 See Chapter 3, Section E.

20 *Ward*, above note 1.

21 See Mullan, above note 15 at 116.

22 *Ibid.*

23 *Ward*, above note 1 at para 58.

claims involving misdeeds by Crown prosecutors. This standard has been lowered somewhat in the case of Crown prosecutors who wrongfully fail to make full disclosure of relevant information.[24] But in other areas of Crown activity involving a high degree of discretion, the *Henry v British Columbia (AG)*[25] case appears to retain the very high standard of malice, and in the *Ward* decision, the Chief Justice suggested that malice might be the appropriate standard.[26]

As for the possibility of *per se* liability or *per se* damages, whether nominal, modest, or substantial, application of the functional test as outlined in *Ward* would seem to rule out such a possibility. However, the comments of McLaughlin CJ in *Henry* suggest that *Charter* damages may be awarded by a court when the claimant has suffered no personal injury or harm if the court considers it necessary to give effect to the vindication or deterrence function of that remedy.[27]

Although many of the negative factors described by Professor Mullan are still having an effect, there are a few hopeful signs to consider. The pre-*Ward Charter* damages success rate of 35 percent and its potential psychological and educational effect on state officials and, to a lesser extent, on potential *Charter* claimants should not be ignored even though that effect is hard to measure. The apparent sharp increase in the number of *Charter* claims for damages in the short post-*Ward* period is another positive sign. If this trend continues, it could be considered evidence of the positive impact provided by the approach to *Charter* damages outlined in *Ward*, an approach that provides all concerned with a clearer understanding of the principles that should underlie an award for *Charter* damages.

C. WHAT THE FUTURE HOLDS

The fact is, however, that the first thirty-three years of *Charter* experience suggests that *Charter* damages awards have had only a modest impact on *Charter* litigation and the enforcement of *Charter* rights. But we should keep in mind that evolution in the natural world takes millions of years. Similarly, the development and evolution of basic legal principles and concepts is laboriously slow. The evolution of *Charter* damages in the future may not

---

24 See *Henry v British Columbia* (AG), 2015 SCC 24 [*Henry*].

25 *Ibid.*

26 *Ward*, above note 1 at para 43.

27 *Henry*, above note 24 at para 117, citing *Ward*, above note 1 at para 30.

be laboriously slow, but if the comments of Moldaver J in *Henry* reflect the preferred approach, it will certainly be incremental.[28]

Thirty-three years is a relatively short time on the evolutionary scale. The full potential of *Charter* damages may yet be revealed. One post-*Ward*[29] commentator saw that potential as rather limited, describing the impact of *Ward* and its future effect as "largely symbolic and ornamental."[30] Hopefully the impact of *Ward* on *Charter* damages as a constitutional remedy will prove to be more significant and evolution will continue. Only time will tell.

---

28 *Henry*, above note 24 at para 35.

29 *Ward*, above note 1.

30 Allen M Linden, "*Charter* Damage Claims: New Dawn or Mirage?" (2012) 39:4 *The Advocates' Quarterly* 426 at 439.

Appendices

Appendix 1

Master List of *Charter* Damages Cases

1984–2015

A. 1984–94

1) *Crossman v Canada*, [1984] 1 FC 681, 12 CCC (3d) 547, [1984] FCJ No 61 (TD). Trial court awarded $500 punitive damages.
2) *Collin v Lussier*, [1983] 1 FC 218, 6 CRR 89, [1983] FCJ No 35 (TD), rev'd in part (1984), [1985] 1 FC 124, 22 CCC (3d) 124, [1984] FCJ No 195 (CA). Trial court awarded $18,136 ($10,636 compensatory and $7,500 punitive damages); overturned by Court of Appeal.
3) *Vespoli Precision Mechanics Ltd v Canada* (1984), 12 CRR 185, 55 NR 269, [1984] FCJ No 709 (CA). Trial court rejected *Charter* damages claim; affirmed by Court of Appeal.
4) *S Bertram Miller Ltd v Canada*, [1985] 1 FC 72, 18 DLR (4th) 600, [1985] FCJ No 61, rev'd [1986] 3 FC 291, 28 CCC (3d) 263, [1986] FCJ No 404 (CA), leave to appeal to SCC refused (1986), 75 NR 159n. Trial court awarded $13,349 compensatory damages; overturned by Court of Appeal.
5) *Lagiorgia v Canada*, [1985] 1 FC 438, 18 CRR 348, [1985] FCJ No 74 (TD), rev'd in part [1987] 3 FC 28, 57 CR (3d) 284, [1987] FCJ No 438 (CA), leave to appeal to SCC refused (1988), 61 CR (3d) xxviii, 43 CCC (3d) vi, 33 CRR 372n. Trial court rejected *Charter* damages claim; affirmed by Court of Appeal.
6) *Scorpio Rising Software Inc v Saskatchewan* (AG) (1986), 46 Sask R 230, [1986] SJ No 295 (QB). Trial court rejected *Charter* damages claim.

7) *R v BB* (1986), 69 AR 203, [1986] AJ No 384 (Prov Ct). Trial court awarded $3,000 ($2,250 compensatory and $750 punitive damages).
8) *Breen v Saunders* (1986), 71 NBR (2d) 404, [1986] NBJ No 961 (QB). Trial court rejected *Charter* damages claim.
9) *Lord v Allison* (1986), 3 BCLR (2d) 300, [1986] BCJ No 3205 (SC). Trial court awarded $6,065, composed of $65 special damages, $4,500 general damages ($1,000 of which can be described as *per se* damages), and $1,500 punitive damages.
10) *Crown Trust Co v Ontario* (1986), 54 OR (2d) 79, 26 DLR (4th) 41, [1986] OJ No 2374 (Div Ct). Divisional Court rejected *Charter* damages claim.
11) *Charters v Harper* (1987), 79 NBR (2d) 28, [1987] NBJ No 1150 (QB). Trial court rejected *Charter* damages claim.
12) *Bauder v Wilson* (1988), 43 CRR 149, [1988] BCJ No 1561 (SC). Trial court rejected *Charter* damages claim.
13) *Moore v Ontario (AG)*, [1990] OJ No 3433 (Dist Ct). Trial court rejected *Charter* damages claim.
14) *R v F(RG)* (1991), 90 Nfld & PEIR 113, 5 CRR (2d) 62, [1991] NJ No 20 (SC). Trial court awarded $1,000 punitive damages.
15) *Rollinson v Canada*, [1991] 3 FC 70, 40 FTR 1, [1991] FCJ No 25 (TD); (1994), 20 CCLT (2d) 92, 73 FTR 16, [1994] FCJ No 50 (TD). Trial court awarded $8,000 compensatory damages.
16) *Freeman v West Vancouver (District)*, 1991 CanLII 2365 (BCSC), rev'd (1992), 19 BCAC 81, 71 BCLR (2d) 387, [1992] BCJ No 2146 (CA), leave to appeal to SCC refused with costs (1993), 77 BCLR (2d) xxxi. Trial court awarded $5,000 punitive damages; overturned by Court of Appeal.
17) *Blouin v Canada* (1991), 51 FTR 194, [1991] FCJ No 1171 (TD). Trial court awarded $5,000 compensatory damages.
18) *Lewis v Burnaby School District No 41* (1992), 71 BCLR (2d) 183, [1992] BCJ No 1568 (SC). Trial court awarded $10,000 compensatory damages.
19) *Stenner v British Columbia (Securities Commission)* (1993), 23 Admin LR (2d) 247, [1993] BCJ No 2359 (SC), aff'd (1996), 141 DLR (4th) 122, 82 BCAC 124, [1996] BCJ No 3015 (CA). Trial court rejected *Charter* damages claim; affirmed by Court of Appeal.
20) *McGillivary v New Brunswick* (1993), 140 NBR (2d) 365, 26 CR (4th) 371, [1993] NBJ No 514 (QB), aff'd (1994), 116 DLR (4th) 104, 1994 CanLII 4465 (CA). Trial court rejected *Charter* damages claim; affirmed by Court of Appeal.
21) *Patenaude v Roy* (1994), 23 DLR (4th) 78, 1994 CanLII 6107 (Que CA). Trial court awarded $50,000 compensatory damages; increased to $100,000 by Court of Appeal (additional $50,000 representing punitive damages).

B. 1995–2010

22) *Persaud v Donaldson* (1995), 130 DLR (4th) 701, 25 OR (3d) 270, [1995] OJ No 2284 (Gen Div), rev'd (1997), 143 DLR (4th) 326, 32 OR (3d) 349, [1997] OJ No 542 (Div Ct). Trial court awarded $3,700; overturned by Divisional Court.
23) *Shewfelt v Canada* (1996), 77 BCAC 308, [1996] BCJ No 1368, 1996 CanLII 2700 (CA); (1997), 28 BCLR (3d) 340, [1997] 4 WWR 292, [1997] BCJ No 518 (SC). Court allowed a pre-trial Crown motion to strike plaintiff's claim for *Charter* damages; overturned by Court of Appeal and action allowed to proceed. When the case was heard on its merits, the trial court applying *Schachter* rule rejected *Charter* damages claim.
24) *Wilson Estate v Canada (AG)* (1996), 25 BCLR (3d) 181, 37 CRR (2d) 344, [1996] BCJ No 1264 (SC). *Charter* damages claim based on allegation of wrongful death rejected. No specific *Charter* section invoked by claimant.
25) *Swidzinski v Saskatchewan Power Corp* (1997), 161 Sask R 179, [1997] SJ No 676 (QB). Trial court rejected *Charter* damages claim.
26) *R v Yang* (1997), 35 OR (3d) 109, 43 OTC 382, [1997] OJ No 3802 (Gen Div). Trial court awarded damages representing the value of goods seized.
27) *Walker v Ontario* (1997), 32 OTC 19, 40 CCLT (2d) 197, [1997] OJ No 3343 (Gen Div). Trial court rejected *Charter* damages claim.
28) *R v Hill* (1997), 148 DLR (4th) 337, [1997] 10 WWR 691, [1997] BCJ No 1255 (CA). Trial court rejected *Charter* damages claim; overturned by Court of Appeal, which awarded $500 general compensatory damages.
29) *Krznaric v Chevrette* (1997), 154 DLR (4th) 527, 48 OTC 85, [1997] OJ No 4712 (Gen Div). Trial court awarded $12,773 compensatory damages.
30) *Chrispen v Prince Albert (City) Police Department* (1997), 148 DLR (4th) 720, [1997] 8 WWR 190, [1997] SJ No 360 (QB). Trial court awarded $500 compensatory damages against each of six defendants, for a total of $3,000, and $300 special damages.
31) *Alford v Canada (AG)* (1997), 31 BCLR (3d) 228, [1997] BCJ No 251 (SC). Trial court rejected *Charter* damages claim.
32) *Oniel v Toronto (Metropolitan) Police Force* (1998), 75 OTC 241, [1998] OJ No 3840 (Gen Div). Trial court rejected *Charter* damages claim.
33) *Thompson v Ontario* (1998), 113 OAC 82, 56 CRR (2d) 112, [1998] OJ No 3917 (CA). Court of Appeal rejected *Charter* damages claim.
34) *Jane Doe v Toronto (Metropolitan) Commissioners of Police* (1989), 58 DLR (4th) 396, 48 CCLT 105 (Ont HCJ), aff'd (1990), 74 OR (2d) 225, 72 DLR (4th) 580, [1990] OJ No 1584 (Div Ct), leave to appeal to CA refused (1991), 1 OR (3d) 416, [1991] OJ No 3673 (CA); (1998), 39 OR (3d) 487, 126 CCC (3d) 12, 1998 CanLII 14826 (Gen Div). Court rejected a Crown motion to strike claim for declaration and damages, alleging negligence and violation of *Charter* rights;

affirmed by Divisional Court. When the case was heard on its merits, the trial court found breach of *Charter* rights, issued a declaration, and awarded $220,364 plus the present-value sum required to produce $2,000 annually for fifteen years in tort damages but denied the claim for *Charter* damages to avoid double recovery.

35) *Pack MJ Inc v Canada*, [1998] FCJ No 1922 (CA). Court of Appeal rejected *Charter* damages claim.
36) *Glover v Magark*, [1999] BCJ No 472 (SC). Trial court rejected *Charter* damages claim.
37) *Westwell v Waterloo (Region) Police Services Board*, [1999] OJ No 1245 (Gen Div). Trial court rejected *Charter* damages claim.
38) *Chua v MNR* (2000), [2001] 1 FC 641, [2000] FCJ No 1812 (TD). Trial court rejected *Charter* damages claim. No specific *Charter* section invoked by claimant.
39) *McTaggart v Ontario*, [2000] OTC 855, [2000] OJ No 4766 (SCJ). Trial court awarded $230,000 ($210,000 compensatory and $20,000 punitive damages) for six years of unlawful confinement.
40) *Ayangma v Prince Edward Island*, 2000 PESCTD 74. Trial court awarded $7,500 compensatory damages.
41) *Sens v Dobko*, 2000 SKQB 589. Trial court rejected *Charter* damages claim.
42) *Dulude v Canada* (1997), 138 FTR 301, [1997] FCJ No 1516 (TD), rev'd [2000] 1 FC 545, 2000 CanLII 16085 (CA). Trial court rejected *Charter* damages claim; overturned by Court of Appeal, which awarded $10,000 damages.
43) *Pinnock v Ontario*, [2001] OJ No 2921 (SCJ). Trial court rejected *Charter* damages claim.
44) *Auton (Guardian ad litem of) v British Columbia (Minister of Health)*, 2001 BCSC 220, var'd 2002 BCCA 538, rev'd 2004 SCC 78. Trial court awarded the four adult claimants $20,000 each, for a total of $80,000; affirmed by Court of Appeal; overturned by Supreme Court of Canada.
45) *Smith v Canada (AG)*, 2001 NBQB 256. Trial court rejected *Charter* damages claim.
46) *Neufeld v Manitoba*, 2001 MBQB 201, aff'd but not on damages issue 2002 MBCA 123. Trial court rejected plaintiff's *Charter* damages claim in a class action and his motion for summary judgment. The Court of Appeal rejected the plaintiff's appeal regarding the dismissal of the motion for summary judgment but restored the plaintiff's action for damages.
47) *Bond v Ontario*, [2002] OTC 658, [2002] OJ No 3499 (SCJ). Trial court rejected *Charter* damages claim.
48) *King v Ontario (Ministry of the AG)*, [2002] OTC 956, [2002] OJ No 4766 (SCJ). Trial court awarded $1,000 compensatory damages.

49) *MacPhee v Ottawa Police Services Board*, [2003] OTC 850, [2003] OJ No 3786, 2003 CarswellOnt 3670 (SCJ). Trial court rejected *Charter* damages claim.
50) *Ilnicki v MacLeod*, 2003 ABQB 465. Trial court awarded $5,000 for breach of *Charter* rights and $6,000 for pain and suffering, a consequence of unnecessary force used during a strip search, for a total of $11,000 compensatory damages.
51) *Euteneier v Lee*, [2000] OTC 833, [2000] OJ No 4533 (SCJ), rev'd in part (2003), 113 CRR (2d) 44, [2003] OJ No 4239 (Div Ct), aff'd (2005), 77 OR (3d) 621, [2005] OJ No 3896, 2005 CanLII 33024 (CA). Trial court rejected *Charter* damages claim; overturned in part by Divisional Court; Court of Appeal rejected *Charter* damages claim.
52) *Ernst v Quinonez*, [2003] OTC 847, [2003] OJ No 3781 (SCJ). Trial court rejected *Charter* damages claim.
53) *MacAlpine v Ontario Progressive Conservative Party*, 2003 CanLII 38584 (Ont Div Ct). Divisional Court rejected claimant's action for *Charter* damages of $2.5 million.
54) *Morin v Prince Edward Island Regional Administrative Unit #3 School Board*, 2004 PESCTD 1, var'd 2005 PESCAD 14. Trial court awarded $15,000 compensatory damages; appeal court increased the award to $75,000.
55) *Chmielewski v Niagara (Regional Municipality) Police Services Board*, [2004] OJ No 3073, [2004] OTC 646 (SCJ), and [2007] OJ No 3052 (SCJ). Trial court rejected *Charter* damages claim.
56) *Mundulai v Wilson*, [2005] OTC 532, [2005] OJ No 2656 (SCJ). Trial court rejected *Charter* damages claim.
57) *Ding v Canada*, 2005 FC 442. Trial court rejected *Charter* damages claim.
58) *B(B) (Litigation Guardian of) v Saint John (City)*, 2005 NBQB 425. Trial court awarded $3,362 compensatory damages.
59) *Bevis v CTV Inc (cob ATV/CTV)*, 2004 NSSC 247, var'd 2006 NSCA 56. Trial court, in a jury trial, awarded each of the two claimants $1,500 compensatory damages, for a total of $3,000; Court of Appeal remitted the case back to the trial court with instructions to instruct the jury more fully.
60) *Pearson v Canada*, 2006 FC 931, aff'd 2007 FCA 380, leave to appeal to SCC refused, [2008] SCCA No 299. All three levels of court rejected *Charter* damages claim.
61) *Samimifar v Canada (Minister of Citizenship and Immigration)*, 2006 FC 1301, aff'd 2007 FCA 248. Trial court rejected *Charter* damages claim; affirmed by Court of Appeal.
62) *Heroux v Toronto Police Services Board*, [2006] OJ No 5190 (Sm Cl Ct). Small Claims Court awarded $7,500 compensatory damages.

63) *Curry v Canada*, 2006 FC 63. Trial court awarded $10,000 compensatory damages.
64) *Ferri v Ontario* (AG), [2006] OJ No 710 (SCJ), var'd 2007 ONCA 79. Trial court and Court of Appeal rejected *Charter* damages claim.
65) *Hawley v Bapoo* (2005), 76 OR (3d) 649, [2005] OTC 894, [2005] OJ No 4328 (SCJ), var'd 2007 ONCA 503; (2006), 82 OR (3d) 382 (SCJ) (costs), var'd 2007 ONCA 503. Trial court awarded $2,500 compensatory damages against each of two defendants, for a total of $5,000; overturned by Court of Appeal.
66) *Radovici v Toronto Police Services Board* (2007), 86 OR (3d) 691 (SCJ). Trial court awarded $7,500 compensatory damages.
67) *Khalil v Canada*, 2007 FC 923, aff'd 2009 FCA 66. Trial court and Court of Appeal rejected *Charter* damages claim.
68) *JL v Gingues*, 2007 QCCS 3276. Trial court rejected *Charter* damages claim.
69) *Ward v Vancouver (City)*, 2007 BCSC 3, aff'd 2009 BCCA 23, var'd (*sub nom Vancouver (City) v Ward*) 2010 SCC 27. Trial court awarded the claimant $5,000 damages for an improper strip search, $5,000 damages for wrongful imprisonment, and $100 damages for wrongful seizure of the claimant's car; affirmed by Court of Appeal. Supreme Court of Canada upheld the award for the improper strip search, noted that the $5,000 award for wrongful imprisonment was not at issue, and rejected the lower courts' $100 award for wrongful seizure of the claimant's car.
70) *Trociuk v British Columbia* (AG), 2008 BCSC 1597. Trial court rejected *Charter* damages claim.
71) *Lahaie v Canada* (AG) (2008), 303 DLR (4th) 213; 63 CCLT (3d) 199, [2008] OJ No 5276 (SCJ), rev'd 2010 ONCA 516, leave to appeal to SCC refused, [2010] SCCA No 371. Trial court awarded $100,000 damages; overturned by Court of Appeal.

C. POST-*WARD* CASES 2010–15

72) *Vancouver (City) v Zhang*, 2010 BCCA 450, supplementary reasons 2011 BCCA 138. Trial court rejected plaintiff's request for declaration of invalidity and damages; affirmed by Court of Appeal applying *Schachter* rule.
73) *Gendreau v Alberta (Department of Justice)*, 2010 ABQB 781. Pre-trial application by plaintiff to amend pleadings to allege breach of ss 7 and 11(d) *Charter* rights rejected for lack of sufficient facts to support a cause of action.
74) *Wiese v Martin*, 2011 SKQB 296. Trial court rejected *Charter* damages claim because not available against individuals and because no breach of *Charter* was proven.

75) *Magiskan v Thunder Bay (City) Police Services Board*, 2011 ONSC 7334. Trial court rejected *Charter* damages claim because no breach of *Charter* was proven.
76) *DWH v DJR*, 2011 ABQB 608. Trial court rejected plaintiff's request for declaration of invalidity and damages, finding this was not an appropriate case for damages.
77) *Gladue v Alberta* (*AG*), 2011 ABQB 651. Trial court rejected *Charter* damages claim; no proof of breach.
78) *Hamalengwa v Bentley*, 2011 ONSC 4145. Pre-trial motion to strike statement of claim for *Charter* damages accepted because no breach of *Charter* was proven and because wrong party was sued.
79) *Dixon v Hamilton (City) Police Services Board*, [2011] OJ No 3836 (SCJ). Trial court rejected *Charter* damages claim; overlap with tort claim.
80) *Russell v York (Regional Municipality) Police Services Board*, 2011 ONSC 4619. Trial court rejected *Charter* damages claim because no breach of *Charter* was proven.
81) *Elliot v Waterloo (Regional Municipality) Police Services*, 2011 ONSC 6889. Trial court awarded $32,000 for breach of *Charter* rights.
82) *R v Wetzel*, 2011 SKPC 9, rev'd 2012 SKQB 24, rev'd in part 2013 SKCA 143. Trial court awarded $5,000 for breach of *Charter* rights; overturned on appeal.
83) *Young v Ewatski*, 2012 MBCA 64, leave to appeal to SCC refused, [2012] SCCA No 440. Trial court rejected *Charter* damages claim because no breach of *Charter* was proven; affirmed by Court of Appeal on different grounds: wrong party sued.
84) *Leroux v Canada* (*Revenue Agency*), 2010 BCSC 865, aff'd 2012 BCCA 63. Trial court and Court of Appeal rejected *Charter* damages claim because no breach of *Charter* was proven.
85) *Sivia v British Columbia* (*Superintendent of Motor Vehicles*), 2012 BCSC 1030, aff'd 2014 BCCA 79, aff'd (*sub nom Goodwin v British Columbia* (*Superintendent of Motor Vehicles*)) 2015 SCC 46. Trial court and Court of Appeal rejected claim. Plaintiff failed to prove bad faith, and *Schachter* rule prevented awarding both a declaration and *Charter* damages. Supreme Court of Canada affirmed lower-court decisions to reject claim.
86) *Conway* (*Re*), 2012 ONCA 519. Court of Appeal held that the Ontario Review Board lacked jurisdiction to grant the plaintiff the remedy requested under s 24(1).
87) *Podolski v Cadillac Fairview Corp*, 2012 ONCJ 545. *Charter* claim rejected because not applicable to non-governmental entities.
88) *Brazeau v Canada* (*AG*), 2012 FC 648. *Charter* claim rejected because no proof of breach.

89) *Forrest v Ontario Provincial Police*, 2012 ONSC 429 (Div Ct). Trial court and appeal court rejected *Charter* damages claim because no bad faith and because no breach of *Charter* was proven.

90) *Lobo v Carleton University*, 2012 ONSC 254, aff'd 2012 ONCA 498. *Charter* claim rejected because not applicable to non-governmental entities; affirmed by Court of Appeal.

91) *R v Reinhart*, 2012 SKQB 95. Provincial Court awarded $500; overturned by appeal court because no jurisdiction in provincial criminal court to award damages.

92) *Lamka v Waterloo (Regional Municipality) Police Services Board*, [2012] OJ No 5591 (Sm Cl Ct). Small Claims Court awarded $5,000 for unwarranted strip search.

93) *Henry v British Columbia* (AG), 2012 BCSC 1401; 2013 BCSC 665, rev'd 2014 BCCA 15, aff'd 2015 SCC 24. After a pre-trial Crown motion to strike *Charter*-based cause of action was rejected, trial court allowed plaintiff to amend pleadings to allege non-malicious acts; overturned by Court of Appeal. Supreme Court of Canada affirmed trial court decision.

94) *Bilich v Toronto (City) Police Services Board*, 2013 ONSC 1445. Pre-trial Crown motion to strike *Charter* damages claim because plaintiff failed to allege bad faith, *mala fides*, or improper purposes rejected by court.

95) *Mason v Turner*, 2014 BCSC 211. Trial court awarded $500 damages for breach of s 10(b).

96) *Gilbert v Canada* (AG), 2014 NBQB 194. Trial court applied functional approach and rejected *Charter* damages claim alleging breach of ss 7, 8, and 11(d).

97) *Everett v McCaskill*, 2014 MBQB 185. Trial court rejected *Charter* damages claim alleging breach of ss 8, 9, & 10(b); bad faith fault threshold not met; no malicious prosecution claim.

98) *VAS v Edmonton (City) Police Service*, 2014 ABQB 666. Trial court rejected *Charter* damages claim because plaintiff did not plead a violation of s 15 and because there was no evidence of breach.

99) *Mallett v McCaskill*, 2014 MBQB 227. Trial court rejected *Charter* damages claim because not available against individuals.

100) *Adamson v Ontario*, 2014 ONSC 3787. Trial court rejected *Charter* damages claim because not available against individuals.

101) *Ernst v EnCana Corp*, 2014 ABCA 285, leave to appeal to SCC granted, [2014] SCCA No 497. Court of Appeal rejected *Charter* damages claim because limitation of action provision (*Energy Resources Conservation Act*, RSA 2000, c E-10, s 43) precluded recovery.

102) *Ontario Society for the Prevention of Cruelty to Animals v Hunter*, 2014 ONSC 6084. Trial court applied functional approach and rejected *Charter* damages claim.

103) *Barton v Nova Scotia* (AG), 2014 NSSC 192. Trial court rejected *Charter* damages claim based on alleged psychological stress because stress must be serious and profound; no violation of s 7.

104) *British Columbia Civil Liberties Assn v University of Victoria*, 2015 BCSC 39. Trial court rejected *Charter* damages claim because not applicable to non-governmental entity performing private actions.

Appendix 2

Number of Cases by Jurisdiction

1984–2014

Jurisdiction	Number of cases	Percentage
Ontario	38	37%
British Columbia	19	18%
Federal	16	15%
Alberta	7	7%
Saskatchewan	7	7%
New Brunswick	6	6%
Manitoba	4	4%
Quebec	2	2%
Nova Scotia	2	2%
Prince Edward Island	2	2%
Newfoundland and Labrador	1	1%
Total	**104**	**100%**

Appendix 3

Relevant Supreme Court of Canada Decisions

1984–94

R v Big M Drug Mart Ltd, [1985] 1 SCR 295.

R v Mills, [1986] 1 SCR 863.

R v Rahey, [1987] 1 SCR 588.

R v Gamble, [1988] 2 SCR 595.

Nelles v Ontario, [1989] 2 SCR 170.

McKinney v University of Guelph, [1990] 3 SCR 229.

Schachter v Canada, [1992] 2 SCR 679.

R v Potvin, [1993] 2 SCR 880.

RJR – MacDonald Inc v Canada (AG), [1994] 1 SCR 311.

Appendix 4

Relevant Supreme Court of Canada Decisions

1995–2010

Weber v Ontario Hydro, [1995] 2 SCR 929.
Guimond v Quebec (AG), [1996] 3 SCR 347.
Blencoe v British Columbia (Human Rights Commission), 2000 SCC 44.
Ontario v 974649 Ontario Inc, 2001 SCC 81.
Mackin v New Brunswick (Minister of Finance), 2002 SCC 13.
Nova Scotia (Workers Compensation Board) v Martin, 2003 SCC 54.
Doucet-Boudreau v Nova Scotia (Minister of Education), 2003 SCC 62.
R v Demers, 2004 SCC 46.
Kingstreet Investments Ltd v New Brunswick (Finance), 2007 SCC 1.
R v Ferguson, 2008 SCC 6.
Ravndahl v Saskatchewan, 2009 SCC 7.

Appendix 5

Final Damages Awards (Trial and Court of Appeal)

1984–2010

Case	Case no.*	Final damages award	Notes
Crossman v Canada	1	$500	
R v BB	7	$3,000	
Lord v Allison	9	$6,000	
R v F(RG)	14	$1,000	
Rollinson v Canada	15	$8,000	
Blouin v Canada	17	$5,000	
Lewis v Burnaby School District No 41	18	$10,000	
Patenaude v Roy	21	$100,000	Trial award of $50,000 increased to $100,000 by Court of Appeal.
R v Yang	26	Value of goods	
R v Hill	28	$500	
Krznaric v Chevrette	29	$12,773	
Chrispen v Prince Albert (City) Police Department	30	$3,300	
McTaggart v Ontario	39	$230,000	
Ayangma v Prince Edward Island	40	$7,500	
Dulude v Canada	42	$10,000	

Case	Case no.*	Final damages award	Notes
Auton (Guardian ad litem of) v British Columbia (Minister of Health)	44	$80,000	Award reversed by SCC.
King v Ontario (Ministry of the AG)	48	$1,000	
Ilnicki v MacLeod	50	$11,000	
Morin v Prince Edward Island Regional Administrative Unit #3 School Board	54	$75,000	Trial award of $15,000 increased to $75,000 by Court of Appeal.
B(B) (Litigation Guardian of) v Saint John (City)	58	$3,362	
Bevis v CTV Inc (cob ATV/ CTV)	59	$3,000	Jury award; sent back by Court of Appeal for reconsideration of award.
Heroux v Toronto Police Services Board	62	$7,500	
Curry v Canada	63	$10,000	
Radovici v Toronto Police Services Board	66	$7,500	
Ward v Vancouver (City)	69	$10,100	Trial award affirmed by Court of Appeal; reduced to $10,000 by SCC.

* See Appendix 1 on page 131.

Appendix 6

Trial Court Awards

1984–2010

Case	Case no.*	Award	Notes
Crossman v Canada	1	$500	
Collin v Lussier	2	$18,136	Reversed on appeal.
S Bertram Miller Ltd v Canada	4	$13,349	Reversed on appeal.
R v BB	7	$3,000	
Lord v Allison	9	$6,000	
R v F(RG)	14	$1,000	
Rollinson v Canada	15	$8,000	
Freeman v West Vancouver (District)	16	$5,000	Reversed on appeal.
Blouin v Canada	17	$5,000	
Lewis v Burnaby School District No 41	18	$10,000	
Patenaude v Roy	21	$50,000	Increased to $100,000 on appeal.
Persaud v Donaldson	22	$3,700	Reversed on appeal.
R v Yang	26	Value of goods	
Krznaric v Chevrette	29	$12,773	
Chrispen v Prince Albert (City) Police Department	30	$3,300	
McTaggart v Ontario	39	$230,000	
Ayangma v Prince Edward Island	40	$7,500	
Auton (Guardian ad litem of) v British Columbia (Minister of Health)	44	$80,000	Affirmed on appeal; reversed by SCC.
King v Ontario (Ministry of the AG)	48	$1,000	
Ilnicki v MacLeod	50	$11,000	
Morin v Prince Edward Island Regional Administrative Unit #3 School Board	54	$15,000	Increased to $75,000 on appeal.
B(B) (Litigation Guardian of) v Saint John (City)	58	$3,362	

Case	Case no.[*]	Award	Notes
Bevis v CTV Inc (cob ATV/ CTV)	59	$3,000	Jury award; sent back by Court of Appeal for reconsideration of award.
Heroux v Toronto Police Services Board	62	$7,500	
Curry v Canada	63	$10,000	
Hawley v Bapoo	65	$5,000	Reversed on appeal.
Radovici v Toronto Police Services Board	66	$7,500	
Ward v Vancouver (City)	69	$10,100	Affirmed on appeal; reduced to $10,000 by SCC.
Lahaie v Canada (AG)	71	$100,000	Reversed on appeal.

* See Appendix 1 on page 131.

Note: As the above list shows, trial awards were affirmed or increased by provincial appeal courts in four cases (numbers 21, 44, 54, and 69) and reversed in six cases (2, 4, 16, 22, 65, and 71). In two cases (21 and 54), the appeal court increased the trial award.

Appendix 7

Court of Appeal Decisions

1984–2010

Case	Case no.*	Award	Trial decision
Collin v Lussier	2	None	Reversed.
Vespoli Precision Mechanics Ltd v Canada	3	None	Affirmed.
S Bertram Miller Ltd v Canada	4	None	Reversed.
Crown Trust Co v Ontario	10	None	Affirmed.
Freeman v West Vancouver (District)	16	None	Reversed.
Stenner v British Columbia (Securities Commission)	19	None	Affirmed.
McGillivary v New Brunswick	20	None	Affirmed.
Patenaude v Roy	21	Damages	Affirmed and damages increased.
Persaud v Donaldson	22	None	Reversed.
R v Hill	28	Damages	Reversed.
Thompson v Ontario	33	None	Affirmed.
Pack MJ Inc v Canada	35	None	Court of Appeal decision only, no trial decision.
Dulude v Canada	42	Damages	Reversed.
Auton (Guardian ad litem of) v British Columbia (Minister of Health)	44	Damages	Affirmed; reversed by SCC.
Euteneier v Lee	51	None	Affirmed.
Morin v Prince Edward Island Regional Administrative Unit #3 School Board	54	Damages	Affirmed and damages increased.
Bevis v CTV Inc (cob ATV/CTV)	59	Damages	Affirmed. (Court of Appeal sent case back for reconsideration of award.)
Pearson v Canada	60	None	Affirmed.
Samimifar v Canada (Minister of Citizenship and Immigration)	61	None	Affirmed.

Case	Case no.*	Award	Trial decision
Ferri v Ontario (AG)	64	None	Affirmed.
Hawley v Bapoo	65	None	Reversed.
Khalil v Canada	67	None	Affirmed.
Ward v Vancouver (City)	69	Damages	Affirmed; $100 award reversed by SCC, leaving $10,000.
Lahaie v Canada (AG)	71	None	Reversed.

* See Appendix 1 on page 131.

Appendix 8

Cases Involving Section 7 or 8 of the *Charter*

1984–94

Case	Case no.*
Section 7	
Collin v Lussier	2
Breen v Saunders	8
R v F(RG)	14
Rollinson v Canada	15
Stenner v British Columbia (Securities Commission)	19
McGillivary v New Brunswick	20
Section 8	
Vespoli Precision Mechanics Ltd v Canada	3
S Bertram Miller Ltd v Canada	4
Lagiorgia v Canada	5
Scorpio Rising Software Inc v Saskatchewan (AG)	6
R v BB	7
Rollinson v Canada	15
Patenaude v Roy	21

* See Appendix 1 on page 131.

Appendix 9

Compensatory Damages Awards

1984–94

Case	Case no.*	Compensatory trial award	On appeal
Collin v Lussier	2	$11,000	Reversed.
S Bertram Miller Ltd v Canada	4	$13,349	Reversed.
R v BB	7	$2,250	
Lord v Allison	9	$4,500	
Rollinson v Canada	15	$8,000	
Blouin v Canada	17	$5,000	
Lewis v Burnaby School District No 41	18	$10,000	
Patenaude v Roy	21	$50,000	Affirmed.

* See Appendix 1 on page 131.

Appendix 10

Punitive Damages Awards

1984–94

Case	Case no.*	Punitive trial award	On appeal
Crossman v Canada	1	$500	
Collin v Lussier	2	$7,500	Reversed.
R v BB	7	$750	
Lord v Allison	9	$1,500	
R v F(RG)	14	$1,000	
Freeman v West Vancouver (District)	16	$5,000	Reversed.
Patenaude v Roy	21	None	$50,000 punitive damages added.

* See Appendix 1 on page 131.

Appendix 11

Rejected Claims

1984–94

Case	Case no.*	Trial court	Appeal court
Collin v Lussier	2		x
Vespoli Precision Mechanics Ltd v Canada	3	x	x
S Bertram Miller Ltd v Canada	4		x
Lagiorgia v Canada	5	x	x
Scorpio Rising Software Inc v Saskatchewan (AG)	6	x	
Breen v Saunders	8	x	
Crown Trust Co v Ontario	10		x
Charters v Harper	11	x	
Bauder v Wilson	12	x	
Moore v Ontario (AG)	13	x	
Freeman v West Vancouver (District)	16		x
Stenner v British Columbia (Securities Commission)	19	x	x
McGillivary v New Brunswick	20	x	x

* See Appendix 1 on page 131.

Appendix 12

Cases Where a High Standard of Fault Was Required

1984–94

Case	Case no.*	Award	Qualified immunity defence
Collin v Lussier	2	$18,136; reversed on appeal	Raised but not applied by trial court.
Lagiorgia v Canada	5	None	Raised and applied by trial and appeal courts.
Scorpio Rising Software Inc v Saskatchewan (AG)	6	None	Raised and applied by trial court.
Crown Trust Co v Ontario	10	None	Raised and applied by trial and appeal courts.
Moore v Ontario (AG)	13	None	Not clear whether it was raised by the defence.
Stenner v British Columbia (Securities Commission)	19	None	Raised and applied by trial and appeal courts.
McGillivary v New Brunswick	20	None	Argued and applied by trial and appeal courts.

* See Appendix 1 on page 131.

Note: The high standard of fault required by the courts in these cases involved malice, bad faith, or improper motive.

Appendix 13

Cases Where a Lower or Non–*Mala Fides* Standard of Fault Was Applied

1984–94

Case	Case no.*	Award	Standard of fault
Crossman v Canada	1	$500	Intentional tort standard applied.
Vespoli Precision Mechanics Ltd v Canada	3	None	Tortious act required.
S Bertram Miller Ltd v Canada	4	$13,349; reversed on appeal	No fault required.

Case	Case no.*	Award	Standard of fault
R v BB	7	$3,000	Tortious act involved; no discussion of fault standard.
Breen v Saunders	8	None	Tortious acts committed; no discussion of fault re *Charter* damages because of tort-and-*Charter* conflict.
Lord v Allison	9	$6,000	Court indicated negligence would be sufficient and even misadventure would suffice.
Charters v Harper	11	None	Tortious acts committed; no discussion of fault re *Charter* damages because of tort-and-*Charter* conflict.
Bauder v Wilson	12	None	Tortious acts committed; no discussion of fault re *Charter* damages because of tort-and-*Charter* conflict.
R v F(RG)	14	$1,000	Court declared negligence or carelessness would be sufficient.
Rollinson v Canada	15	$8,000	Tortious acts committed claimed sufficient.
Freeman v West Vancouver (District)	16	$5,000; reversed on appeal	Tortious acts committed.
Blouin v Canada	17	$5,000	No fault required.
Lewis v Burnaby School District No 41	18	$10,000	Error committed; no other fault.
Patenaude v Roy	21	$50,000; increased to $100,000 on appeal	Intentional tortious acts committed.

* See Appendix 1 on page 131.

Appendix 14

Rejected Claims (Trial and Court of Appeal)

1995–2010

Case	Case no.*	Trial court	Court of Appeal
Persaud v Donaldson	22		x
Shewfelt v Canada	23	x	
Wilson Estate v Canada (AG)	24	x	
Swidzinski v Saskatchewan Power Corp	25	x	
Walker v Ontario	27	x	
Alford v Canada (AG)	31	x	
Oniel v Toronto (Metropolitan) Police Force	32	x	
Thompson v Ontario	33	x	x
Jane Doe v Toronto (Metropolitan) Commissioners of Police	34	x	
Pack MJ Inc v Canada	35	x	x
Glover v Magark	36	x	
Westwell v Waterloo (Region) Police Services Board	37	x	
Chua v MNR	38	x	
Sens v Dobko	41	x	
Pinnock v Ontario	43	x	
Smith v Canada (AG)	45	x	
Neufeld v Manitoba	46	x	
Bond v Ontario	47	x	
MacPhee v Ottawa Police Services Board	49	x	
Euteneier v Lee	51	x	x
Ernst v Quinonez	52	x	
MacAlpine v Ontario Progressive Conservative Party	53	x	
Chmielewski v Niagara (Regional Municipality) Police Services Board	55	x	
Mundulai v Wilson	56	x	
Ding v Canada	57	x	
Pearson v Canada	60	x	x
Samimifar v Canada (Minister of Citizenship and Immigration)	61	x	x

Case	Case no.*	Trial court	Court of Appeal
Ferri v Ontario (AG)	64	x	x
Hawley v Bapoo	65		x
Khalil v Canada	67	x	x
JL v Gingues	68	x	
Trociuk v British Columbia (AG)	70	x	
Lahaie v Canada (AG)	71		x

* See Appendix 1 on page 131.

Appendix 15

Successful Claims (Trial and Court of Appeal)

1995–2010

Case	Case no.*	Trial court	Court of Appeal	Award	Notes
R v Yang	26	x		Value of goods	
R v Hill	28		x	$500	
Krznaric v Chevrette	29	x		$12,773	
Chrispen v Prince Albert (City) Police Department	30	x		$3,300	
McTaggart v Ontario	39	x		$230,000	
Ayangma v Prince Edward Island	40	x		$7,500	
Dulude v Canada	42		x	$10,000	
Auton (Guardian ad litem of) v British Columbia (Minister of Health)	44	x		$80,000	Award reversed by SCC.
King v Ontario (Ministry of the AG)	48	x		$1,000	
Ilnicki v MacLeod	50	x		$11,000	
Morin v Prince Edward Island Regional Administrative Unit #3 School Board	54	x	x	$15,000	Increased to $75,000 on appeal.

Case	Case no.*	Trial court	Court of Appeal	Award	Notes
B(B) (Litigation Guardian of) v Saint John (City)	58	x		$3,362	
Bevis v CTV Inc (cob ATV/CTV)	59	x	x	$3,000	Jury award; sent back by Court of Appeal for reconsideration of award.
Heroux v Toronto Police Services Board	62	x		$7,500	
Curry v Canada	63	x		$10,000	
Radovici v Toronto Police Services Board	66	x		$7,500	
Ward v Vancouver (City)	69	x	x	$10,100	Affirmed on appeal; reduced to $10,000 by SCC.

* See Appendix 1 on page 131.

Appendix 16

Court of Appeal Decisions

1995–2010

Case	Case no.*	Trial decision
Damages denied		
Persaud v Donaldson	22	Reversed.
Thompson v Ontario	33	Affirmed.
Pack MJ Inc v Canada	35	No trial decision.
Euteneier v Lee	51	Affirmed.
Pearson v Canada	60	Affirmed.
Samimifar v Canada (Minister of Citizenship and Immigration)	61	Affirmed.
Ferri v Ontario (AG)	64	Affirmed.
Hawley v Bapoo	65	Reversed.
Khalil v Canada	67	Affirmed.
Lahaie v Canada (AG)	71	Reversed.
Damages awarded		
R v Hill	28	Reversed.
Dulude v Canada	42	Reversed.
Auton (Guardian ad litem of) v British Columbia (Minister of Health)	44	Affirmed; reversed by SCC.
Morin v Prince Edward Island Regional Administrative Unit #3 School Board	54	Affirmed.
Bevis v CTV Inc (cob ATV/CTV)	59	Affirmed. (Court of Appeal sent case back for reconsideration of award.)
Ward v Vancouver (City)	69	Affirmed; $100 award reversed by SCC, leaving $10,000.

* See Appendix 1 on page 131.

Note: In four of the eight cases where the appeal court rejected the *Charter* damages claim, it was affirming the trial court's rejection. In four of the six cases where the appeal court awarded damages, it was affirming the trial court's decision.

Appendix 17

Required Level of Fault in Cases

1995–2010

Case	Case no.*	Level of fault
Persaud v Donaldson	22	Bad faith recognized.
Swidzinski v Saskatchewan Power Corp	25	Negligence claimed but not proven.
Walker v Ontario	27	Tortious act recognized.
Alford v Canada (AG)	31	Some fault recognized.
Oniel v Toronto (Metropolitan) Police Force	32	Bad faith recognized.
Glover v Magark	36	Some fault recognized.
Westwell v Waterloo (Region) Police Services Board	37	Some fault recognized.
Sens v Dobko	41	Malice recognized.
Pinnock v Ontario	43	Malice recognized.
Smith v Canada (AG)	45	Recklessness or *mala fides* recognized.
Bond v Ontario	47	Wilful disregard for plaintiff's rights recognized.
MacPhee v Ottawa Police Services Board	49	Arbitrary conduct recognized.
Euteneier v Lee	51	Bad faith recognized.
Chmielewski v Niagara (Regional Municipality) Police Services Board	55	Malice recognized.
Ding v Canada	57	Bad faith recognized.
Ferri v Ontario (AG)	64	Bad faith recognized.
Hawley v Bapoo	65	Bad faith recognized.
Pearson v Canada	60	Bad faith or abuse of power required by the Court of Appeal.
Samimifar v Canada (Minister of Citizenship and Immigration)	61	Some fault recognized.
JL v Gingues	68	Some fault recognized.
Trociuk v British Columbia (AG)	70	Bad faith recognized.
Lahaie v Canada	71	Bad faith recognized.

* See Appendix 1 on page 131.

Results: A high standard of fault, such as malice, bad faith, arbitrary conduct, or wilful disregard of *Charter* rights, was required in fifteen cases. A lower standard of fault, such as negligence or other tortious conduct, was required (or sufficient) in seven cases.

Appendix 18

Cases Where the Claimant Failed to Prove a *Charter* Violation

1995–2010

Case	Case no.*
Wilson Estate v Canada (AG)	24
Thompson v Ontario	33
Neufeld v Manitoba	46
MacPhee v Ottawa Police Services Board	49
MacAlpine v Ontario Progressive Conservative Party	53
Mundulai v Wilson	56
JL v Gingues	68

* See Appendix 1 on page 131.

Appendix 19

Number of Cases by *Charter* Section

1995–2010

Section	Number of cases
2	0
3	6
4	0
5	4
6	0
7	20
8	12
9	13
10	3
11	4
12	1
13	0
14	1
15	10

Appendix 20

Cases Involving Section 9 of the *Charter*

1995–2010

Case	Case no.*
Walker v Ontario	27
Chrispen v Prince Albert (City) Police Department	30
Sens v Dobko	41
Bond v Ontario	47
King v Ontario (Ministry of the AG)	48
MacPhee v Ottawa Police Services Board	49
Ernst v Quinonez	52
Chmielewski v Niagara (Regional Municipality) Police Services Board	55
Mundulai v Wilson	56
Bevis v CTV Inc (cob ATV/CTV)	59
Heroux v Toronto Police Services Board	62
Radovici v Toronto Police Services Board	66
Ward v Vancouver (City)	69

* See Appendix 1 on page 131.

Appendix 21

Non-*Charter* Cases Where the *Ward* Test for Damages Was Applied

Arunachalam v Best Buy Canada, 2010 HRTO 1880.

De Abreo v Humber Institute of Technology & Advanced Learning, 2010 HRTO 2404.

Nammo v TransUnion of Canada Inc, 2010 FC 1284 (federal *Privacy Act*).

Palangio v The Corporation of the Town of Cochrane, 2011 HRTO 1491.

Canada (AG) v Tipple, 2011 FC 762 (labour law).

AL v CC, 2011 ABQB 819 (family law).

Girao v Zarek Taylor Grossman Hanrahan LLP, 2011 FC 1070 (federal *Privacy Act*).

Thibodeau v Air Canada, 2011 FC 876 (*Official Languages Act*).

Appendix 22

Use of *Charter* Section 24 Remedies

1984–2007

	1984–94	1995–2007	Total	Percent-age of total
Section 24(1) remedies	193	724	917	
stay of proceedings	54	522	576	63.0%
miscellaneous judicial orders	59	47	106	12.0%
declaration of *Charter* breach	48	45	93	10.0%
legal costs	11	62	73	8.0%
damages	21	48	69	7.5%
Section 24(2) exclusion of evidence	63	854	917	

Note: Data regarding stays of proceedings, miscellaneous judicial orders, declarations of *Charter* breach, and legal costs under s 24(1) and exclusion of evidence under s 24(2) is derived from the *Charter of Rights Decisions* reporter (Vancouver: Western Legal Publications, 1982) (loose-leaf). Data regarding the number of damages claims under s 24(1) is derived from Appendix 1.

Index

About the Author

Professor W.H. Charles received his LLM from Harvard University and Michigan Law School. In 1983, he was appointed as a Queen's Counsel, and in 2001 he received his LLD (Hon) from Dalhousie University. After teaching at Dalhousie Law School for over thirty years, he became Dean of the Faculty of Law. After retiring from teaching full-time, he was appointed as professor emeritus at the Dalhousie Law School. Professor Charles has written several books and articles, particularly with reference to personal injury damages. He has held numerous prestigious positions on various commissions and boards, including serving as president of the Law Reform Commission of Nova Scotia and chair of the Nova Scotia Environmental Assessment Board.

FSC
www.fsc.org
MIX
Papier | Fördert
gute Waldnutzung
FSC® C083411

Kolibri 360 GmbH
Ferdinand-Jühlke-Straße 7
99095 Erfurt, Deutschland
produktsicherheit@kolibri360.de